The Restaurant Marketing Bible

How to Market Your Restaurant on a Shoestring Budget

Jerry Minchey

Copyright © 2009 Jerry Minchey

Disclaimer and/or legal notices:

Even though all attempts have been made to verify the information provided in this publication, neither the author nor the publisher assumes any responsibility for any errors, inaccuracies or omissions. Any slights of people, organizations or groups are unintentional.

This publication is not intended for use as a source of legal or accounting information and should not be used as such. Competent professionals should be consulted if such services or information is needed. The information in this publication is subject to all federal, state and local laws or regulations. All users of this information must be sure all appropriate laws or regulations are followed.

The author and publisher assume no responsibility or liability whatsoever on behalf of any purchaser, reader or user of this material.

The publisher and author specifically disclaim any liabilities for any loss incurred as a consequence of following any advice or applying information presented in this book.

Acknowledgments

I am indebted to Marilyn Minchey, Patricia Benton, Mitzi Santiago and Brent Minchey without whose help and suggestions this book would not exist.

Table of Contents

The Restaurant Marketing Bible

How to market your restaurant on a shoestring budget

Introduction

Are you ready for a change? Do you long for a restaurant that is highly successful and not sucking the life out of you 12 hours a day 7 days a week? Some restaurant owners have this life. What do they know that you don't know? You are about to find out and it's not as hard to achieve as you think.

There was a bestselling book out recently called *The 4- Hour Work Week,* by Timothy Ferriss. When I went to the book store and asked the clerk if they had the book, she jokingly asked, "Would that be in the fiction or the humor section?"

Maybe it's not fiction or humor. Is it possible to run a highly successful restaurant and work only four hours a week? I doubt it, but bringing customers into your restaurant is the most important part of your job and this book can make the four hours a week you spend on marketing into your most effective and productive time.

Hard work alone won't make your restaurant super successful and highly profitable. If it did, you would already have a highly profitable restaurant.

To be super successful in the restaurant business you have to:

Dream
Plan
Make it Happen

1

I'm sure you have done the dreaming. You have imagined the lifestyle you want and the kind of super successful restaurant you want. In the rest of this book I'm going to show you how to "Plan" and then how to "Make it happen." Let's get started.

Note: If you read this book cover to cover, you may notice some redundancy. That's because I understand that most busy people don't have time to read an entire book in one sitting and you may choose to read the sections first that are most interesting to you.

Because of this, I have tried to make each section stand alone without the necessity of constantly referring from one section to another. My aim is to provide a user friendly guide that is easy to navigate, understand, and implement.

You will also notice that I have used bold to emphasize some sections of the text in this book. I did this because I know your time is valuable and I want you to be able to quickly find sections you want to read again. As you read this book, have your yellow marker close by and highlight ideas you want to implement. Then frequently go back and review the sections you have highlighted.

In other words, you will find a few statements and concepts repeated in different sections of this book. I did this so the sections could stand alone and, after all, some of these statements are profound and are worth reading two times.

## Chapter 1

Your Marketing Plan

Spending 7% of your gross sales on marketing or 5% more than you spent last year is not a marketing plan. And listening to every smooth-talking, high-pressure ad salesman who walks in making grand promises and then writing checks to the ones who make the wildest promises is even worse. Unfortunately, these are the two most popular restaurant marketing plans in the industry today.

But maybe it's not so unfortunate after all. Let your competition keep doing that while you implement a proven marketing plan that will. . .

Drive a starving crowd to your restaurant while slashing thousands of dollars from your marketing and advertising budget.

And to make it even better, this plan will also free up about 70% of the time you have been working.

The key is to work **"on** your restaurant and **not** in** your restaurant."

Start every day with the one statement and one question below clearly in your mind. Type it up and post it on your bathroom mirror or on the wall in front of your desk.

Here are the one statement and the one question that will change your restaurant:

> **"I can't make $100,000 a year doing $10 an hour work."**

> **"What can I do in four hours today that will contribute more to the success of my restaurant than anything else I can do?"**

Think about how much of your long day now is being spent doing $10 an hour work and then remember that your time should be spent marketing your restaurant. You can hire managers and workers to do everything else. You may think you can't afford to hire managers to manage the routine things, but you could if you spent a little more time marketing your restaurant.

The only way left for the little guy to get rich in the restaurant business is to have a competitive advantage.

You can't have the best chef. You can hire the best chef in town from a competitor, but another competitor can (and probably will) steal him away from you.

You can't have the best location. You could have the best location for a short time, but road construction, new building projects, population shifts all combine to turn your best location into less than an ideal location for your restaurant.

You can't have the best menu – at least, not for long. Your favorite recipes can be copied and maybe even improved upon.

You can't be the cheapest. That's the worst way of all to try to make money in the restaurant business. There will always be someone with lower prices. (They're probably going out of business. . . they just don't know it yet.) Try to compete with them and you may go out of business before they do.

There are only three real and sustainable competitive advantages you can have in the restaurant business:

Innovation

Marketing

You

Taking advantage of these three things is **the only way left for the little guy to get rich in the restaurant business.**

Peter Drucker (the greatest management author and guru of all time) said, **"Innovation is the only lasting competitive advantage you can ever have in any business."** He's right. "Marketing" and "You" are just sub-parts of "Innovation."

McDonald's founder, Ray Kroc said, "We can innovate faster than the competition can copy."

Marketing is the only thing that generates profit for your business. **Everything else is an expense**. And to be cost effective your marketing has to be innovative. You can't just do what every other restaurant is doing – or you will end up just like they are–barely getting by.

Marketing (when done right) is the best investment you can ever make. In the stock market or in real estate you may hope for a 5% or maybe even a 20% return on your investment, but in marketing, a $100 investment in promotion (ads, direct mail, press releases, etc.) can bring you $1,000 in profit and sometimes much more.

For example, changing the headline in an ad could bring you two to 10 times more profit from the same ad. And the only cost to you to make the change is the time it took you to learn how to write headlines. What kind of return on investment is that?

The only thing in your entire business that cannot be copied or stolen is YOU.

The average restaurant owner or manager thinks his job is to "run the restaurant." He doesn't have time to market (or even to learn how to market) his restaurant. Maybe that's why he's average.

Most restaurant owners work long hours, but it doesn't take long hours to market, innovate and promote your restaurant.

I stopped by to see a restaurant owner the other day. His business was going down the tubes and he was back in the kitchen peeling potatoes. He said, "I have put my heart and soul into this restaurant. If it doesn't make it, it's not because I haven't put the hours in." He thought that as long as he was working hard and staying busy, he was doing all he could do. He's not alone. A lot of restaurant owners and managers fall into this mindset.

Stop doing the $10 an hour work and concentrate on doing what you and you alone can do to make your restaurant successful. Then you will discover that **marketing is the only way left for the little guy to get rich in the restaurant business.**

Imagine the feeling you will have when you master the concept of **innovation, marketing and you.** When you do this you

5

will know that you could swap restaurants with any restaurant owner in town – Let him have your location, your menu, your chef and your staff and in less than a year you could have a more profitable restaurant than he has–because he doesn't have YOU.

I was talking to a friend recently who has been following the advice in this book. He took over as manager of a failing restaurant about six months ago and last week when he was in the grocery store the owner of a competing restaurant came up to him and said, "I hear that you're the restaurant turnaround king. How about coming to work for me?" Follow the advice in this book and you will soon have that reputation.

Bottom line: Don't chase the so-called competitive advantages that are short-lived and non-sustainable. **Concentrate on: Innovation, Marketing and You.**

## Chapter 2

Your Unique Selling Proposition – USP

The next step in your marketing plan should be to decide what's unique about your restaurant. In what way is your restaurant better than or different from your competition?

Can you answer this in one or two sentences? If you can't, you're not alone: the owners of most average restaurants can't either. Of course, that's why their restaurants are average. You can bet the really successful restaurant owners can answer the question, and soon you'll be able to answer it too.

The answer to this question in marketing terms is what is called your **Unique Selling Proposition or USP**.

You have to come up with the answer to this before you can even start to do any effective advertising. One of the main reasons to advertise is to get this message across to your customers and prospects.

Your USP should tell people why they would enjoy coming to your restaurant more than they would if they went to eat at one of your competitors. Your USP should also tell them why they should come eat at your restaurant instead of staying home and watching Law and Order reruns on TV.

The USP of most restaurants is either: "Me, too" or "We specialize in everything."

Of course, no restaurant actually says this, but in a roundabout way that's what their ads are saying. And that's the message their potential customers are getting.

I'm sure you've seen ads that say something like, "We specialize in steaks, seafood, pasta," and on and on and then say, "we have the fastest service and the lowest prices and the best location, etc."

You can't be all things to all people. That's like taking a yellow marker and highlighting every word on a page. You haven't emphasized everything. You have emphasized nothing.

If your ad looks like all the other ads, you're saying, "Me, too." You might as well make this your headline. "We're just like every other pizza restaurant."

Some restaurants do a good job of getting their USP across. I'm sure you know what Domino's USP is: **"Fresh, hot pizza delivered to your door fast."** Getting this USP across to their potential customers is what made the founder a millionaire. He didn't claim to have the best pizza.

Notice that Domino's USP doesn't say anything about being the best pizza or about an old world recipe, etc.— just hot and fast.

Papa John's, on the other hand, claims to have the freshest and best ingredients. If you watch their TV commercials, you will quickly see what their USP is.

While we're discussing pizza, do you know what Pizza Hut's USP is? Pizza Hut claims to be "America's favorite pizza."

The USP for Federal Express is, "If it absolutely, positively has to be there overnight."

Okay, now that you realize that coming up with your USP is important, the question is, "How do I do it?"

In other words, how do you find out or decide what's great about your restaurant? Why do people come to your restaurant? What should you be promoting? It's probably not what you think.

You can't be objective about your restaurant. You don't see what your customers see. You've been buried in it for too long.

A friend of mine bought a used car a while back. The first time I took a ride with him, the first thing I saw was some cracked, discolored after-market plastic trim on the door panels. It was ugly and made an otherwise nice car look cheap. When I commented on it, he said he was planning to have the cracked plastic trim removed immediately.

The other day when I rode with him, I noticed the cracked plastic trim was still there. I said, "I thought you were going to get that replaced." He said he kept putting it off until it was convenient and then he'd gotten so used to the ugly, discolored and cracked plastic trim that he didn't even see it anymore—and he'd owned the car for two years. He had totally forgotten about it.

How many good or bad things are there in your restaurant that you no longer see?

Of course, you can't answer that question because you don't know how many things you don't see.

On the other hand, what are the really good things about your restaurant? You've seen that wonderful view for so long you take it for granted. And you've eaten your she-crab soup (that you used to think was wonderful) for so long you're tired of it. You may be wondering, "Is it really all that good?"

You can't answer any of these questions. You can't be objective about your own restaurant. It's not because you are being biased or unrealistic, it's because your mind tunes out most of the good and the bad.

You could ask some of your friends, but do you think they would really tell you if they thought your food was awful? Or they may be like you and have been there so much they don't see things either.

You could put a stack of comment cards in the lobby. With comment cards you would mostly get comments from your really unhappy customers. This is always good information, but it doesn't tell you the full story. What about the little nagging things that people don't complain about?

You could consider hiring a professional "Mystery Diner" to evaluate your restaurant. Some of these services are good, but others are not. Get some referrals (hopefully from someone you know) before you hire a service.

The best way for you to find out what's really special about your restaurant and also what's bad about your restaurant is to get "real comments" from your customers.

By real comments, I mean comments where the customer puts a LOT of thought into them – Where the customer is racking his or her brain and really trying to tell you what you need to do to make your restaurant their favorite of all the restaurants in town.

Hold a contest for 30 days and give away free dinners for two (complete with dessert and a bottle of wine) to the winners.

Ask everyone who comes in to fill out a short form answering three questions. On the form, state that there will be two first place winners. There will be one winner for the most helpful answers and another first place winner for the most creative answers. Each first place winner will receive a free dinner for two (complete with a dessert and a bottle of wine.)

Here are the three questions to ask:

Question #1: What 3 things do you like best about this restaurant?

Question #2: What are the 3 things you dislike most about this restaurant?

Question #3: Other than correcting the things that you don't like, what 3 ideas can you give me about what I can do to make this your favorite restaurant in the galaxy?

On the form be sure to have a place for their name, address, birthday (month and day only), anniversary, email address, mailing address and phone number.

In addition to getting some great ideas that you would never have thought of, you will also get to add a lot of names to your data base.

I would suggest you mail or email an announcement to each person who entered the contest and tell him or her who won in each category. Tell them that their ideas were great also, and that they won a second prize of a free dessert with each entrée or even a free dinner for one.

Here is another technique to help you select a USP for your restaurant. It won't get you as many good ideas as the above exercise, but it is quick and easy to implement.

The first step is to focus on the one little need, niche or gap that is sorely lacking in your market. (Of course, it has to be one that you can fulfill.)

Start by asking your customers why they came to your restaurant. That will give you some ideas of what they think your USP is. They may be coming for a reason you haven't thought of. Consider it. Is it because of your location, view, food, live music or what?

Write down what's good about your restaurant and what's bad about your competition. Get out two pieces of paper and on one sheet write down everything that's unique or great about your restaurant. On the other sheet write down everything that's bad about, or not being done correctly, by your competitors. This exercise should show you your strong points and your competitor's weak points. This will give you some ideas to work with. If you don't know your main competitor's strong and weak points, go eat there and see what you can find out.

Go to the library and **look at the restaurant yellow page ads in other cities** and see what stands out as a promise or USP for other restaurants. Don't just look at ads for your type of restaurant. Look at all of them. Of course, don't expect to find many really good examples, but you'll find some.

Don't try to be funny or cute. I saw a yellow page ad for a plumbing company that said, "Don't sleep with a drip. Call a plumber." A muffler shop ad said, "No appointment necessary. We'll hear you coming." Humor almost never works for a USP. It's tempting sometimes to use humor, but don't.

Your logo is not your USP. Logos don't sell. No one except you and your mother care about your logo.

What if your restaurant really is just like every other restaurant and there's nothing unique about it?

What can you do? You can **imply** that there's something better and unique about your restaurant.

Consider this example. I'm not a big fan of hot sauces, but if I did like hot sauce, I would buy Pace Picante Sauce. All picante sauces taste pretty much the same, but Pace makes their sauce in Texas and their main competitor makes their sauce in New York.

Pace's USP is, "We're from Texas where picante sauce originated. Now you tell me – who's going to make a better

11

picante sauce. A bunch of New York sissies or some Texas guys who know what picante sauce is all about?"

They didn't say their picante sauce was the best, but they sure made me believe it was. I'm sure you've seen these TV commercials.

If you had a pizza restaurant, you could say, "Why settle for some assembly line fast food pizza chain's pizza that tastes like cardboard, when you could have the original old world (or Chicago or New York) style pizza made with real cheeses and fresh ingredients in a real wood-fired brick oven?"

You didn't say the other guys didn't use real cheeses or that they didn't use fresh ingredients, but you implied it. As a lawyer would say, you gave the jury a cause for reasonable doubt.

Negative campaigning in politics usually doesn't work and it usually doesn't work in advertising either – in fact, it could backfire on you. Here's a better way to do it.

Instead of saying the competition does X and you do Y, you can say, "the industry standard is X and we do Y." Compare yourself to the industry standard. Yea, I know. There isn't an official industry standard, but in most cases there is a standard or typical way things are done.

For example, you can say, "The industry standard is to wash fruits and vegetables only one time, but we wash and inspect ours three times."

Here are some sample successful USPs for you to consider and to get you thinking:

You can mix and match these points and change the words to fit your situation and come up with the perfect USP for your restaurant.

USP Examples

- Voted the area's best seafood restaurant six years in a row.
- We wash and inspect our fruits and vegetables three times to ensure that only the cleanest and best produce is served.

- Great food. Cool drinks. And one terrific view.
- Fine dining in a casual atmosphere with the best water view and sunset view in the area.
- When the occasion demands the very best
- The only classic German cuisine in town.
- Mexican on the Marina - live music and great views.
- We're the only seafood restaurant with our own shrimp boat. It doesn't get any fresher than this.
- Pizza from the Old World – fresh from our own wood-fired brick oven.
- Not only the best, but the largest pizzas in town.
- The most delicious specialty pizzas in town made with healthy ingredients and spring-water dough.
- Fresh from our docks to your table. We have our own shrimp and fishing boats and we have the finest waterfront sunsets.
- Authentic French dining plus, French chef, Olivier, on classical guitar.
- You won't find a more enjoyable, relaxing, romantic atmosphere anywhere else.
- When we cater your wedding (or any event), you won't run out of food or be disappointed in any way or everything's free – Guaranteed!
- Voted the best place for an evening out – no exceptions. Our number one goal is to keep our title.
- The best Mexican food in town or it's Free!
- The place to take her when you're in the doghouse.
- Lunch in 12 minutes or it's Free!
- The best Japanese fast food in town - Fast, Healthy and Delicious.
- Char-broiled steaks delivered fast and hot to your door.
- Mexican dining with a New England flair.

- Ocean fresh seafood with a Kansas flair.
- The best seafood in town and a fantastic mountain view from every table.

Use the above examples to help you come up with the perfect Unique Selling Proposition for your business. Modify and substitute words until you get the strongest USP possible for your restaurant.

Most of the above examples are only one sentence, but your USP can be more than one sentence. A one sentence USP is great if you can do it. Keep it to one very short paragraph at the most or no one will remember it.

Here are some more ideas to help you come up with your USP

Many restaurants are now seeing 10% to 15% decreases in business from the same period last year, while others are having their best growth ever.

In general the restaurants that are doing the same things they have always done are the ones having problems – and it may get worse.

Read the book, *Who Moved My Cheese*. Just because your marketing techniques have always worked, doesn't mean they'll continue to work in the future. The needs and wants of the marketplace have changed and your competition has probably changed.

Also, a lot of areas have been over-built with restaurants during the last few years and now there's going to be a weeding out period.

The **innovative** restaurants will survive while restaurants that cling to the past and with no clear USP will struggle or worse.

Here are two things that will help define your USP in the minds of your customers:

1. Differentiate your restaurant

If you showed your mother pictures of the inside of 10 restaurants, could she pick out your restaurant? The inside of a lot of restaurants look almost identical – make sure that doesn't describe your restaurant.

When you differentiate your restaurant you can bring in more customers **and** raise prices at the same time.

2. You need a clear theme throughout your restaurant

All of your marketing needs to reflect this theme. You can't be all things to all people. Most people go to a restaurant time after time for one reason and one reason only. That reason should be your USP.

I used to go to a mom and pop diner for breakfast three or four mornings a week. You can't do much to bacon, eggs, grits and toast to make them different, but the experience was unique. Decorations didn't make it unique – it was the friendliness and the "Cheers bar" atmosphere of the place.

Take a look at this picture:

Illustration 1: Fiddlin' Pig Restaurant in Asheville, NC

Is there any doubt what the theme of this restaurant is? This is an example of **differentiation** and **innovation**. Of course, this theme wouldn't go over in many places, but in Asheville, North Carolina it's going over big. I was there recently on a Wednesday night and I had to wait 30 minutes to get a table. Not bad for a Wednesday night.

You don't have to change the theme of your restaurant. Just decide what the theme of your restaurant is and enhance it.

If you have a seafood restaurant, when a customer sits down, does he get the feeling, he's on the dock of a New England fishing village (or some other seafood theme)? A few fishing nets hung on the wall won't do it.

Enhancing the theme of your restaurant is relatively inexpensive and it pays big rewards when it comes to differentiating your restaurant from all the other restaurants in town.

If your restaurant's not special in some way, there's no reason for people to come and there's really no reason for them to come back.

Here's what one restaurant did that made them special, got them a ton of free publicity and didn't cost them a dime.

Take a look at this picture. This may be too informal for your restaurant (with paper towels hanging above each table on a coat hanger and dollar bills stapled to the wall), but it sure works for this restaurant in Indian Rocks Beach, Florida.

Illustration 2: P.J.'s restaurant in Indian Rocks Beach, FL

As an added bonus, the restaurant gets a **lot** of free publicity (with feature articles in the local newspapers) because every six months they donate all of the dollar bills to the local Children's Hospital.

Last year they gave over $10,000 to the local Children's Hospital. You better believe that will get you a top-of-the-page story and a picture in your local papers.

All of the walls, posts, etc. are covered with dollar bills that people put up wishing someone a happy birthday or a happy anniversary, etc. Sometimes everyone in a birthday party will put up a dollar bill wishing the "birthday person" a happy birthday.

The bills stay up for six months before they're donated to the hospital. People like to come back and sit in the booth that has the dollar bills with their birthday wishes written on them.

To make things even more informal, there are signs on the walls with sayings like:

- "Courteous service available upon request."
- "If you don't like the way I run this place, buy me out."
- "Don't feed the owner. He's too fat already."

I was there recently on a Sunday night with some friends. We got there a little after 9:00 P.M. and the place was packed. The food was great and the service was extremely fast.

Most of the other restaurants in the area were dead that late on a Sunday night. It looks like this restaurant has found a way to be special.

Coming up with your USP and conveying it to your prospects and customers in every aspect of your marketing is your most powerful advertising weapon.

Most of your competitors don't have a USP. They try to be everything to everyone. Having a USP and using it in all of your marketing will deliver a real knock-out blow to your competitors. They won't know what hit them.

Don't spend another dime on advertising until you have a USP. Absolutely nothing is as important to your success as selecting the right USP.

After you come up with your USP, it's very important that every member of your staff knows your USP by heart.

Stop members of your staff from time to time and ask them, "What is our USP?" Word will get around that knowing the restaurant's USP is important to the boss. It won't help much if you are the only one who knows what your USP is.

Look at it this way. A compass is more important than a stopwatch on any journey because it's more important to be going in the right direction than it is to going fast and making good time. Your USP is your compass.

Chapter 3

The Three Parts of Marketing

Now that you have selected your USP, the next step is to take a look at what I call the three "M" parts of marketing. The three "M" parts are. . .

Message, Market, and Media

First, Your Message: "What would you say to someone if you had 30 seconds to convince them to come to your restaurant?"

In marketing terms this is called your "elevator pitch." In other words, if you were on an elevator and you had a chance to explain to someone why they should dine in your restaurant, but you had to do it before they got off at the next floor, what would you say?

In a nutshell, your elevator pitch is your main marketing message. That's the message you would like every one of your staff and your current and potential customers to know.

Next, Your Market: Who would you tell this message to? Once you know what you want to say, who needs to hear it?

Who are your potential customers? A hint, they're probably mostly just like your existing customers. Find out where your existing customers live, find out where they work, what they do for a living and for fun. Find out as much as you can about your existing customers to find out who your most likely new customers will be.

Finally, Your Media: What media should you use to reach these new customers? If you know what you would say to a potential customer and you know who and where these people are, what would be the best advertising media to use to get this message to the people you have identified as your most likely potential customers?

Most restaurant owners get the cart before the horse, and select the media (TV, newspaper, etc.) to use without ever thinking much about whom they are trying to reach.

If you find out that most of your potential customers live within a two-mile radius of your restaurant, would it make sense to pay for a TV or newspaper ad that covers the whole city with a population of 100,000 or more?

If you stopped and didn't read another word in this book and just implemented what has been covered so far, you would have a better and more cost effective marketing program than 99% of the independent restaurants in the galaxy – but we're just getting started.

Here's one more thing for you to consider and when it comes to advertising, this should be your motto:

Track it or Trash it

Apply this one concept to ALL of your advertising expenses and your restaurant WILL be profitable. This is the biggest secret of successful restaurant owners.

This simple technique will quickly show you which advertising programs to drop. Then eliminate the advertising money that is being wasted on ineffective advertising programs and the money that is being spent on advertising programs that you don't know whether they're working or not. All of the money saved will go straight to the bottom line. Continue with only the advertising programs that you **know for sure** are working. Of course, this may eliminate all of your present advertising, but that's okay for now. Just do it.

Even more important, by eliminating the wasted advertising money, you will free up money for truly effective advertising.

Baseball managers and baseball fans are the only people who track statistics and data more than restaurant owners. Restaurant owners track food cost and average ticket amount, how the sales were vs. this day last year, etc. They track everything. . . EXCEPT their advertising campaign results.

Track ad results for only ONE day and you will know more about what's working and what's not working than 90% of your competitors.

You don't have to take a month to come up with an elaborate data gathering and tracking system. (In Chapter 6 we will talk about how to track your ad results on an ongoing basis and provide you a sample form to collect these data.)

But for now, just stand at the door one night and greet and welcome every arriving guest. Tell them that you know they had a lot of choices of where to eat tonight and you would like to ask them what was the main reason or reasons they selected your restaurant and then record this data.

If it's a busy night, you could drop a little tape recorder in your shirt pocket or coat pocket and record the data. You won't get the best sound quality, but it will be easy enough for you to understand and transcribe later.

We talked earlier about only working four hours a day. If you did nothing else today except spend four hours greeting guests and asking this one question, you would know more about what advertising is working for your restaurant and where you're wasting money than probably any other restaurant owner in town.

Now what else is it that you have to do during your next big meal today that is more important than collecting this data?

One restaurant owner did this recently and found out that 98% of his customers were repeat customers and had not seen any of his ads recently. He was spending $20,000 a month on advertising and it was doing almost nothing for him. He needs to do some marketing to bring in new customers to replace the attrition, of course, but what he was doing was a total waste of money.

Bottom line: Collect your data today and start canceling ads tomorrow.

Print and Media Ads:
How, When and If

Print and media ads are where you are probably spending 90% or more of your marketing budget. This is your biggest opportunity to waste money like it's going out of style and most restaurants take advantage of this opportunity. They waste money on ads that are not working. You shouldn't stop marketing, but you should stop wasting money on ads that are not working.

In this chapter I'm going to show you how to do two things:

#1. Cut the cost of your advertising by 50% to 80% or more by paying much less for the same advertising and by eliminating the inefficient and ineffective part of your advertising.

#2. Change your ads to make them pull in 2 to 10 times more business with the same size ad.

Let's start with the **"How"** part of writing and buying media ads and we will get back to the **"When"** and **"If"** later.

Marketing is what makes or breaks any restaurant and a headline is what makes or breaks any ad, sales letter, flier or post card. Since five times as many people read the headline as read the body of any ad, **the most important thing you can do to turn your restaurant into a super-profitable money-making machine is to become a headline expert.** It's a lot easier than you think.

Learn to write and analyze headlines and you will be miles ahead of your competition. How much time do you think your competitors have spent learning about headlines? – Probably zero. That's good news because that means it won't take much effort on your part to be way ahead of them.

I want you to be convinced that the following headline writing techniques work, so let me tell you where this information comes from.

The following information comes from both my personal experiences and from one of the greatest marketers of all time, Ted Nicholas. **Ted has spent over $100,000 million of his own money testing headlines and testing marketing techniques.**

I have studied with him in his home in Switzerland, attended his seminars and tested his marketing techniques for years. If you want the world's two best books on marketing and writing headlines, I suggest you get a copy or two of Ted's many books. The two I recommend are *Magic Words That Bring You Riches* and his new book, *Billion Dollar Marketing Secrets*.

Since the purpose of this section is to help you become a headline writing expert, let's start by asking. . .

How much can you expect a great headline to really do for you?

Eighty percent of the effectiveness of any ad is the headline. I have had ads that pulled 17 times more response by changing the headline.

A 17 times larger response means that instead of getting 10 customers from an ad, you could get 170 or instead of getting 100 you could get 1,700. Even a two or three times increase would make a difference wouldn't it?

How to write headlines

The purpose of a headline is to offer a reward for reading the rest of the ad. It's that simple. Keep this concept in mind and writing headlines will be a lot easier. First, what should a headline accomplish?

In a nutshell, the **first thing a headline has to do is to attract attention**. If no one sees your ad or reads your sales letter or post card or flier, it doesn't matter what it says does it?

Next, your headline should offer an irresistible benefit.

Finally, your headline should answer the question, "What's in it for me?"

Guidelines for writing headlines and what makes a great headline

First of all, your headlines should emphasis a benefit and **not** a feature. A benefit answers the question, "So what?" For example, your restaurant has a fireplace. That's a feature. The fireplace creates a romantic, intimate atmosphere. That's a benefit. Don't get these two things mixed up. Answer the question we talked about earlier, "What's in it for me?" or in other words, "What will I get out of coming to your restaurant?"

A good way to think about how to write a headline is to ask yourself this simple question. . .

"If I had unlimited, magical powers to grant my customers the biggest benefit possible, what would it be?"

In Chapter 2 we spent some time deciding what your Unique Selling Proposition or USP should be. Now we're going to use your USP in your headlines.

As we said in Chapter 2, you can't be all things to all people. Decide what it is that's great and unique about your restaurant and then write a headline promising the greatest benefit you can really deliver. Promote your USP in all of your advertising.

The most important job of your headline is to **trigger an emotion**.

Don't try to sell with logic. Buying decisions are made with emotion first and then just enough logic so the buyer won't look silly when someone asks him/her why they did that or bought that or went there.

Here are the important things to keep in mind when writing your headlines.

Your headline should talk to one person – not to a group. Picture one customer in your mind and write the headline to appeal to that one person.

25

Your promise must not only be true, it must be believable. – "World's best Bar-B-Que" is not believable. "Voted best BBQ in Dallas by the *Dallas Morning News* readers" is believable.

DO NOT USE ALL CAPITAL LETTERS. Do you see how hard this is to read? Graphic designers think it draws attention to the headline. It doesn't. It makes readers skip over it. Capitalize the first letter in the first word or if you have a short headline, capitalize the first letter of each word. People read by scanning and they can't read all upper case words fast. Let your competition keep using all caps.

Don't use reverse type much – if at all. (Reverse type is white letters on a black background.) If you do use reverse type, only do it with two to three words maximum – and then **only** if it is large type. Reverse type is hard to read and most people just skip over it.

Never use more than 17 words in a headline. This number is **not** arbitrary. This has been tested many times. Some of the best headlines of all times have had exactly 17 words, but very few headlines with more than 17 words have ever been successful.

You can use a sub-head in smaller print below a main headline.

Use short, powerful words that bring a picture to mind.

Omit most adjectives and adverbs.

Use strong colorful verbs.

Use present tense.

If you include a picture, use it correctly. If an important benefit of eating in your restaurant can be described by a picture (water view, etc.), you can use a picture for up to 1/3 of your ad. Place the picture at the top of your ad and your headline right **below** the picture. Your headline must support and relate to the picture. Don't have a picture of a water view and a headline about your barbecue ribs.

Do not put your logo or the name of your restaurant at the top of your ad. No one cares about your logo except you and your mother. In most cases a logo doesn't promise a benefit. If you must use your logo, make it small and place it in the bottom corner of your ad.

Don't try to be cute or funny. It can be done, but it almost always fails. Even the experts usually don't risk trying humor. It's not worth it.

Use at least one of these 21 powerful words and phrases in every headline:

- new
- amazing
- at last
- discover
- how would
- hate
- warning
- only
- now

- secrets of
- yes
- love
- bargain
- do you
- advice to
- why
- which
- wanted

And here are the final three and the most powerful words of all time to use in a headline. You can't go wrong when using one of these three:

- free
- how to
- you

Here are variations of the 19 most successful headlines ever written. (I have modified them slightly to fit the restaurant industry, but the concept is the same.). Don't waste another dollar on an ad until you have studied these 19 killer headlines.

Modify these headlines to fit your needs. The good news is that most of these powerful, profit-producing headlines have not been used by your competitors.

These headlines work because they provoke emotions and promise benefits. Human nature and human emotions don't change. Use these all-time proven headlines to spark your imagination to come up with the perfect headline for your restaurant.

Use these headlines word-for-word (except insert your information, of course) or modify them. You can use these headlines to help you get ideas also. Either way, you will get fantastic results.

The purpose of a headline is to get people's attention and to get them to read the next line of the ad, sales letter or postcard. Would the following headlines get your attention?

Killer headlines that get results

- Local Chef swears under oath that he didn't steal his recipes from world famous chefs
- Local seafood restaurant swears under oath that they don't have their own fishing fleet – or. . . their own garden behind the restaurant - or – you get the idea.
- Free Delivery
- She laughed when I suggested Cheryl's Piano Bar for our anniversary, but when the evening was over. . .
- If you were given $1 million to spend, isn't this the kind of restaurant you would build?
- Did you ever see a fat Chinaman? (Ad for a Chinese restaurant getting the message across that Chinese food is healthy and non-fattening.)
- The amazing secrets of a French chef (or - you fill in the blank)
- If you're in the dog-house, bring her to Laura's Steakhouse tonight and you'll be out in no time.
- My accountant said I was crazy to give away a FREE dinner to everyone in Phoenix. (Use this headline with your birthday program.)

- Let us cater your next event and you'll never run out of food or everything is free

- The lazy man's way to host a perfect party or event

- Free dinner for everyone in Atlanta – or – Free dinner. No strings attached. (Use these headlines with your birthday program.)

- Sane talk about why Mexican food is actually healthy and good for you. (You can substitute Chinese, Japanese, Southern cooking or any type of food.)

- The search for the perfect dessert (steak, pizza, lobster, etc.) just ended

- Lunch in 11 minutes or it's Free – Guaranteed

- When the evening has to be really perfect, where would Don Juan go? Sub-head – Recently he chose Jenny's Bistro. Come let us show you why

- You give up things when you come to Jack's Steakhouse. Things like loud noise, bad food, lousy service and high prices

- What makes Antonio's the best Italian restaurant in Dallas? Sub-head – There is really no magic about it – it's merely patient attention to details.

- Warning – Don't eat another steak (or order another pizza, or another shrimp, etc.) before you read this

The above examples should get your creative juices flowing. Don't try to write the perfect headline. Just think about what is unique about your restaurant and write 10 so-so headlines immediately. Then write five more a day for eight days and you'll have 50 great headlines to choose from. You can use some of them for sub-heads.

I doubt if your competition has ever come up with more than one or two headlines to consider for any ad. With your 50 headlines, you will be miles ahead of any competitor.

Never use your logo at the top of your ad or as a headline. Your logo should go in the bottom left or right corner of your ad.

The top of your ad should have a headline that promises a strong benefit and one that answers the questions, "What's in it for me?" In other words, "Why should I eat at your restaurant?" or "Why should I keep reading this ad?"

What about logos?

Logos served a big purpose at one time. Logos were originally useful to develop brand loyalty when many customers couldn't read. People could recognize the box of Morton's salt showing a picture of the little girl with an umbrella or Aunt Jemima's picture on a box of pancake mix.

Today, when you see McDonald's famous "golden arches," you're getting a message. The logo is saying, "Here we are." But. . .

Face it – You DON'T have the budget to get your logo to be well known like McDonald's logo and your logo doesn't say anything anyway. Forget about it.

To make things worse, most logos are designed by a graphic designer trying to use some font style that no one can read. There's no message in most logos and most of the time you couldn't read the message if there was one.

I'm not down on logos. There are a lot of places where you should use your logo. Your logo should be on the front or top of your menus, on your letterhead and business cards and almost everywhere EXCEPT as a headline for your ads.

Yes, you need a good logo for your restaurant (or almost any other business).

By the way, if you don't have a good logo, check out **www.GotLogos.com.** I get all of my logos from Daniel at this site. He is fast and he only charges $25 for a basic logo. If you need a more advanced logo or several logos to choose from, contact Daniel and he will work with you.

Here's another interesting way to get a great logo for very little cost. You've heard the TV commercial that says, "When banks compete, you win." It's about having banks compete for your mortgage business. You can do the same thing with logo designers and have them compete for your logo design business at **99designs.com**

Here's how it works. You sponsor a contest offering $100 (or whatever amount you choose) to the winning design. Several free-lance graphic designers will actually design logos for you to choose from. Of course, the more prize money you offer the winner, the more designers you will have submitting designs for you to choose from and the more effort they will put into their designs.

You will usually get 5 or 10 logos submitted fairly quickly and you select the one you want and award the $100 prize (or whatever amount you said you would pay). Everything is done for you at the above website. It's actually kind of fun to see all the logo designs you get to choose from. Offer $200 or more and you will really get a lot of designs to choose from.

Yes, your business needs a good logo, but trying to use it as a headline to promote your business is costing you dearly.

Immediately move your logo to the bottom of all of your ads and put a strong headline at the top of your ads and watch your response rates really take off.

Some final words of advice about headlines:

Spend a lot of time writing headlines before you decide which one to use. I sometimes write over 100 headlines for an ad. Jot down headlines when they come to you – driving down the road, in the shower or in the middle of the night. Take a few days to come up with your list of headlines.

Don't hire a graphic artist to write or design your ad.
That's one of the biggest mistake most restaurant owners make. (Use them to layout your ad after you have basically designed it if you want to, but keep them on a short leash and don't let them get carried away.)

Graphic artists want to use type styles that can't be read and most of them have never taken a single course on how to write a headline. Many times your message will get lost in their fancy graphics.

Graphics should support the message in the ad – not take away from it. I've seen many ads where the graphics are so over-powering that the message gets lost.

You know your business and your customers. You need to write your own ads. At the very least, you need to write your own headline and sub-heads.

Apply these headline techniques whether you're writing a newspaper ad, a magazine ad, a flier or a brochure.

How to write powerful ad copy

Keep in mind that the headline is 80% of any ad, flier or brochure, so spend spent 80% of your time on the headline. Most people reverse these numbers and spend 20% (if that much) of their time on the headline and 80% on writing the ad – or even worse spend 80% of their time on the graphics.

- Write it like you are talking to **one** person and in the present tense - not the past tense.

- Write short sentences.

- Make use of bullets.

- It's okay to use small text after the headline captures their attention. Don't try to make everything stand out with big print. If you try to emphasize everything, you emphasize nothing.

- Write like you would talk to a friend over a cup of coffee.

- Try to evoke an emotion. Don't try to sell using logic. Buying decisions are made based on emotions and **not** for logical reasons. Use words that paint a picture or conjure up an emotion.

- Don't try to use humor. Yes, humor can work, but it fails more times than it succeeds. Even the highest paid ad writers fail more than they succeed when they try to use humor.

- Be sure to employ the basic AIDA (Attention, Interest, Desire and Action) format when writing your ad and make sure it's not boring and that it flows smoothly.

- Be sure to have a "Call to Action." What is it that you actually want the reader to do? Don't assume that it's clear. State what it is you want the customer to do and state it clearly.

- Of course, be sure to include the name of your restaurant, your address, phone number, website URL and the hours you're open. If it is not clear where you're located from your address, do what it takes to make it clear - include a map or say, "Across the street from the Post Office" or "Southgate Mall" or whatever it takes let people know where you're located.

- Use common everyday words and if you have a question about how which word to use, try using the Google Fight tool at **www.GoogleFight.com/**. For example, should you use *bar-b-que, barbeque, barbecue or BBQ*? Which word is most common? The Google fight tool says that *bar-b-que* is used 2 million times on the Internet, *barbeque* is used 11 million times, *barbecue* is used 33 million times and *BBQ* is used 50 million times. So, if you are going to spell it out, use barbecue, but BBQ is the most common term used.

- And by all means track the results from the ad. Remember your new policy, **Track it or Trash it.**

When and if you should run ads

Now that we've covered the "How" part of How, When and If – Let's talk about the When and IF part of advertising in the print and broadcast media

The best advice comes from Claude Hopkins, one of the greatest marketing people who ever lived and author of the book, *Scientific Advertising*. He said, **"Only advertise when you have news of value."**

If all businesses followed his advice, the newspapers would be almost empty and the radio and TV stations couldn't stay on the air. You don't see or hear very many ads that have any real "news of value."

In other words, don't run an ad that basically says, "I'm still here. Don't forget about my restaurant." I know, no restaurant actually uses those words, but that's the message that comes across to the readers in many cases.

Most media type ads don't work for small independent restaurants. They are a total waste of money. The biggest problem with media type of advertising is that you are paying to cover a large area that is not your potential market. If you were printing fliers and hiring someone to go hang them on doors, you wouldn't tell the person to go hang a flier on every door within a 50-mile radius would you? It's easy to see that the campaign wouldn't pay off, but that's what you're paying for with most newspaper, radio and TV ads.

The single biggest way to save money on restaurant advertising is to totally stop all media advertising.

Now that I've said that, let's talk about when it might be appropriate to do some media type advertising.

First of all, only when you have some news of value – a grand opening, a really big event, your restaurant was just voted as having the best seafood in town, or the most romantic restaurant, etc. and – then **only** if there is a publication that covers just your market area. In other words, is there a Neighborhood Section of the newspaper that only goes to your area, or are you in a small town that has a local paper basically serving just your market?

Some cable TV companies are now offering to show your TV ad only in a small select area. If this service is available in your area, you could give it a try.

Of course, all of the above is assuming that you have a way to track the actual ad campaign to see how it works. Remember the rule for **all** advertising, **Track it or Trash it.** This statement should be stuck on the wall behind your desk and maybe even on your bathroom mirror.

Here is one big exception:

In the restaurant business it is generally accepted that most of your customers will come from within a three to five mile radius of your restaurant. In most cases this is true. **But. . .** if there

34

really is something unique about your restaurant, then you may be able to draw customers from a much larger area.

For example, if you have the only restaurant with live jazz music or the only restaurant with a water view or the only restaurant where you catch your own fish or you are the only restaurant serving all the catfish you can eat, etc., then people will drive 10 to 20 miles or more to get to your restaurant.

In every case mentioned above I have driven 25 miles or more to get to the restaurant described. And I didn't go by myself. In every case a group of us went – sometimes there were two or more cars full of people going for a fun evening.

If you have the kind of restaurant that people will drive 10 or 20 miles to get to, then you could possibly benefit from newspaper ads – **if** you do it right.

You will have "regular" customers coming to your restaurant, but they will be regular in the sense that they may come once a month – not two times a week. When they come it will be an "event" for them. These customers are loyal and they will spread the word about what a great experience it is to eat at your restaurant.

You won't be able to contact these customers by handing out fliers, running ads in your small local paper, etc. This is where an ad in a larger paper could pay off. Since these people will be considering it an event to come to your restaurant, advertise it as an event.

Here is what I have seen work great in this situation. A small ad (two columns wide by three inches high) in the weekend "Entertainment" or "What's Happening" section of a newspaper that covers a wide area pulls in large numbers every week for one restaurant.

Spend the extra money to have the ad in color, but by color I mean make it black print on a yellow background. Have a great headline like, "Live Jazz music Friday and Saturday nights" and of course, don't use your logo as the headline. When you run the ad, track the results like a hawk. If it works keep doing it and if not, trash it immediately.

## Chapter 5

How to Buy Advertising at Discounts Up to 80%

Stop wasting money on advertising by paying more than you have to for your restaurant ads. Let a retired restaurant advertising salesman reveal the inside secrets of how to buy all of your advertising at discounts up to 80% or more. All you have to do is use these three techniques. One of the techniques is to negotiate, but there are two more. These three techniques work every time.

Surprisingly, the restaurants that are struggling the hardest and really need the big discounts are the ones that don't negotiate. . . maybe that's why they're struggling, but negotiating is only part of the technique of buying ads at big discounts.

One thing to keep in mind – Ad salespeople usually need to sell you an ad way more than you need to buy another ad. This is your real "ace in the hole" when it comes to negotiating.

Let's start at the beginning. People selling ads can eat up a lot of your time. Don't let it happen to you.

How to buy an ad in 3 minutes and save 50% to 80% on your ads

Start by saying, "I'm busy. I don't have time to haggle. Give me your bottom line, take it or leave it price. What's the very least you will take for a half-page color ad? (Of course, you're not going to buy at the price he or she quotes, but that will usually cut from 1/3 to 1/2 off the price immediately. THEN you start negotiating from there.)

This is important. Whatever price you are quoted you **gasp** and act shocked and say, "That's WAY out of my range. You've got to do better than that." You then, SHUT UP. The first one to speak loses. The salesperson will always speak up and cut the price even more.

When you have the price down as low as you think you can get it (maybe $995 for a $2,500 ad), say, I'll take the ad and pay you right now if you'll do it for $500." Sales people love to walk out with money. (He or she probably won't take the $500 offer, but more than likely he will make a counter offer with something a little better than $995.)

If money is tight, you can offer half down and half with the ad proof.

After you have the price down as low as possible, work on the terms. Sometimes with small ads it's not worth dragging the payments out, but if money is really tight, it sure is.

You probably don't have an unlimited amount of money to spend on advertising, but if you look at it this way, maybe you do.

If you didn't even have enough money in the bank to pay the light bill tomorrow and a salesman walked in wanting to sell you an ad, he probably wouldn't get very far with you would he? You probably wouldn't give him the time of day.

But think about it. If you could buy ads and pay for the ads after the ad produced a profit for you, you really would have an unlimited amount of money to buy ads with, wouldn't you?

So, after you do everything you can do to get the price down to rock bottom, offer to take the ad if you can pay for it over time after the ad comes out. Many times salespeople will take this offer.

Here's the best deal yet – Get the price of an ad down as low as you can and then pay for it with gift certificates.

For example, you got a $300 ad down to $95 by using all of the negotiating techniques discussed above, and then you could say, "I'll do it if I can pay for it in trade."

You will be surprised at how fast most sales people will take this deal because most companies will let the salesperson keep a major portion of the gift certificates they get. At the very least, you can probably pay for part of the ad with gift certificates.

The $95 gift certificate only costs you about $30 in real dollars, but you just got a $300 ad for $30. That's a 90% savings. I've been happy to take this deal many, many times when I was selling ads to restaurants. To make it even better, data show that only about 80% of gift certificates ever get redeemed.

If your competitor paid $300 for the same ad and you got it for $30, it would be easier to compete with him wouldn't it? If you are spending $30,000 a year on advertising, using these techniques could get your advertising down to $3,000 a year.

You won't get a full 90% discount on every ad, but. . . .

In my years of owning a restaurant marketing company, very seldom did I sell an ad that I wouldn't have been happy to sell for a lot less than what I actually sold it for.

Bottom line:

- Negotiate the price down as low as possible by using the techniques described above.

- Then try to pay for all (or at least part) of the ad with gift certificates.

- Or work on terms. Work out some way to pay for the ad with the profit the ad will bring in. Do this by setting up a monthly payment plan.

- One last point: If the salesperson doesn't accept your low-ball offer, when he or she is ready to leave you can say, "If you end up with space left over, call me and maybe we can do business. This leaves the door open and you may still get a call back accepting your offer or an offer only slightly above your last offer.

Follow these steps and you will be surprised at how often you get ads for 10 cents on the dollar. I know. I sold a lot of ads this way and I allowed my sales people to do the same thing.

In this section we have been talking about negotiating, but negotiating is so important to your business that I want to elaborate some more on negotiating and summarize some of the points we've gone over. I want to show you the real easy way to negotiate.

The very best way to save money in advertising is to negotiate. Some types of ads, may not be negotiable, but most are and there are things you can negotiate on other than price - - things like, ad position, layout fee, a little color in the ad, etc.

Use one of the following 7 statements when a salesperson quotes you a price for advertising and watch the price drop by up to 50% or more.

I know these statements work because restaurant owners and managers used them on me when I was selling ads. I dropped the price almost every time I heard one of the statements.

There's no telling how much of a price reduction you might get if you use all 7 of these techniques instead of just one of them.

My 7 magic negotiating statements

#1 Ask For More Than You Expect to Get

One of the cardinal rules of negotiating is that you should ask the other side for more than you expect to get. Henry Kissinger went so far as to say, "Effectiveness at the conference table depends upon overstating one's demands."

When you sit down with an ad salesperson say, "I'm busy. I've already spent all of my advertising budget and I don't have time to haggle. You've got three minutes to tell me why and how your ad will benefit my business and quote me your best take-it-or-leave-it price."

Of course, you're not going to buy at this price. This is where you START the negotiating.

#2 <u>Always</u> flinch at the first price or proposal

Good negotiators know that you should always flinch with shock and act surprised at the other side's first proposals. Even if the price quoted is half of what you expected, you should still flinch and say, "That's WAY out of my range."

#3 Never Say Yes to the First Offer. It's better to say, "You've got to do better that that."

If you do say yes to the first offer, the other person will know that they quoted you a price that was too low. They may even try to find ways to increase the price. You want the other person to leave feeling that they were lucky to get the money and the deal they got from you.

#4 Never offer to Split the Difference

It's human nature to want to "play fair." Our sense of fair play dictates to us that if both sides give equally then that would be fair. The other side is almost always willing to split the difference, so you should try to get a little better deal than this.

#5 Never Make a Concession When You're Negotiating Unless You Ask for Something in Return

Anytime the other side asks you for a concession in the negotiations, you should automatically ask for something in return. You'll usually get it. What you ask for doesn't have to be of equal value to what you gave up. Just ask for **something**. By asking for a little something in return it makes the other side feel that you just barely gave in.

For example, you can say, I'll agree to that price if you'll place my ad in the top right corner of the page. Or you could say, I'll go along with that price if you'll put a color border around my black and white ad.

#6. "If I could, would you" – "Absent higher authority" and "Converting cash dollars to trade dollars." Here's how to put all three of these powerful negotiating techniques into one sentence.

When you're down to the final negotiations, you can say, "If I could get my (accountant, owner, spouse, or some **absent**

higher authority) to go along with this, how much of that price could you take in trade or gift certificates?

#7 Nibble for More at the End

You can usually get a little bit more even after you have agreed on everything if you will use a technique I call nibbling.

You can say, "You ARE going to place my ad in the top right corner of the page, aren't you?" or "You ARE going to place my ad on the right hand page, aren't you?" or "You are going to give me a 2% discount if I pay you now, aren't you?

The sales person is already thinking about what he is going to do with his commission. The last thing he wants is for this sale to fall through. He will usually give just a little more if you "nibble." Of course, it is important that anything the two of you agree to in the nibbling phase gets written into the ad contract.

Bottom line: Use some or all of the above negotiating techniques and you can easily cut the price you pay for advertising by 50% or more in many cases. As I said at the beginning, most of the time the sales person needs the sale much MORE than you need the ad. You're in control. Take advantage of your situation. A dollar saved on advertising goes straight to your bottom line.

Of course, with a little modification you can use these negotiating techniques will all of your suppliers and in your personal business as well. Negotiating can be fun and very profitable.

In addition to negotiating, one of the best ways to make marketing pay is to be sure you get what you pay for. Let me explain.

28% of ads paid for never run

Yes, a recent study revealed that 28% of restaurant ads paid for never ran or they ran incorrectly.

Solve this problem and you have just cut your advertising expenses by 28%. Here's the simple way to make sure you never pay for another unpublished or incorrect ad. First, you have to recognize the problems which are two-fold:

- Many ads never run or never get published.
- Some ads run, but have major errors that make them almost useless or maybe even harmful to your business.

I know this is true because I recently analyzed some of the advertising expenditures for over 100 restaurants. **I found that on average 28% of the money these restaurants were spending was going down the drain.**

On top of that, almost 90% of restaurant managers never even knew that the ads they had paid for never ran, were never published, or had errors so bad as to make the ads almost totally useless.

Your Yellow Page and newspaper ads will probably run, but there's still a big chance that even these ads will contain errors or run in the wrong section.

Radio and TV ads will probably be correct (because, hopefully, you approved the content of the spot), but these types of ads are notorious for running at the wrong times – after your promotional event is over or not at the prime times you were promised, etc.

Ads in hotel in-room directories, coupon books, fliers, new apartment and new home welcome packages and almost any ad sold by an out-of-town company have proven to be the most likely ads to never get published.

This doesn't mean that you should not run these types of ads. The right ones could bring a big return on your ad investment.

Here are the three simple steps that will solve both of these problems and save you up to 28% on advertising

1. Put someone in charge of tracking all ads.

This person will make sure that all ads run as promised and with no errors. Almost anyone on your staff could do this. Just make sure **someone** is in charge of it.

If you really want to make sure all of your ads run and run correctly, pay the person a bonus based on the money they save you. It also helps if you give this person a title such as, "Media Manager" or "Director of Media Affairs," etc.

The person you assign this job to doesn't have to be someone in management. This task can be a fun and challenging assignment for a young, reliable employee.

Be sure to create an ad logbook or computer file outlining the information and dates for every ad that is supposed to come out.

Of course, carefully check, sign and return all ad proofs promptly and then file them with the ad contracts or insertion orders and make them available to your ad checker and also record the details in the ad logbook for quick reference.

2. Pay for all ads with a credit card

You usually have to pay for advertising before ads run and it could be hard to get your money back from some advertisers if the ad didn't run or was incorrect.

Most reliable companies will accept a credit card as payment. If they won't, think long and hard before you agree to buy the ad.

The advantage of paying for your ads with a credit card is that you can get a full refund when an ad doesn't run. Just tell your credit card company that the product or service was never delivered.

Most credit card companies don't want to get involved in what they call, "quality" issues. If you say the ad ran, but it was incorrect, many credit card companies won't give you a refund, but most ad companies don't know this, so you can bluff.

Tell the advertiser that you will dispute the charge on your credit card and report it as fraud to the credit card company. Companies don't want to lose their credit card processing capabilities, so most will settle the matter when they know you mean business.

Most advertisers are honest, but in many cases they're careless. The ad salesperson might lose the paperwork or doesn't convey all of the details and/or changes about your ad correctly to their ad layout people, etc.

Bring ad errors to the attention of most ad companies and they will do the right thing. Sometimes this means giving you a full refund and sometimes it means running the ad again at no charge with the correct information.

3. Hand-write the following Protection Clause into all of your ad contracts or insertion orders.

"Only run this ad as specified in this contract and on the date (or dates) specified and only run it after I have provided you with a signed copy of the ad proof. Otherwise do not run the ad."

Adding this simple protection clause to your insertion order or advertising contracts gives you a LOT of power when ads are not run correctly. Be sure you and the salesperson both initial the above addition to the contract.

Of course, this puts the monkey on your back to make sure someone carefully checks all ad proofs and returns them on time. Be sure to check dates, phone numbers and other critical information in your ads. After you sign the proof you are stuck with the ad.

Making a change to an ad can be a source of problems. Be sure to check to see that the ad that actually runs is the new ad with the changes. You will be amazed at the number of times your old ad runs instead of the new one with the changes.

In summary:

1. Assign someone to follow-up and verify that all ads run and run as specified.

2. Pay for ads with a credit card.

3. Add the above "Protection Clause" to all of your advertising contracts.

Follow these three steps religiously and you can save a lot on your advertising. All of this previously wasted money is now going straight to your bottom line.

Chapter 6

How to Make Big Money on Your Yellow Page Advertising
(even on a limited budget)

What's wrong with most restaurant Yellow Page ads? The short answer – almost everything.

Are you making any of these six mistakes in your yellow page ads?

Stop making the following six mistakes and increase your response by 500% to 700%.

Most restaurant yellow page ads are basically saying, "Me, too." They give the reader no good reason to visit the restaurant.

Below are the 7 problems with most restaurant yellow page ads:

1. More than 90% of yellow page ads have no headline. Start your ad with a powerful, benefit-driven headline – **NOT your logo** or the name of your restaurant. See the Chapter three about how to write killer headlines and review the 27 most powerful restaurant headlines ever written to get ideas for your headline.

2. Describing features instead of benefits. Having a fireplace is a feature. Being able to enjoy a romantic dinner by the fire is a benefit. Describe all of your features as benefits to your customer. An easy way to design a benefit driven ad is to start with a headline like, "Seven reasons why you should dine at Jill's Steak House tonight" and then go from there.

3. No testimonials. One of the most effective advertising techniques is to use testimonials. Testimonials are believed far more than anything you can say. Getting signed permission and then using the person's real name is the most effective form of testimonial. You almost never see a testimonial in a yellow page ad. Use testimonials and you will have your own gold mine. If your restaurant has been "Voted Best Seafood Restaurant" (or whatever), that's a testimonial. Be sure to say this in your ad.

4. No special offer, incentive or call to action. What do you want the prospect to do? Call and make a reservation, cat breakfast at your restaurant in the morning? Give them a strong incentive to choose your restaurant – maybe a 100% money-back guarantee. Almost no restaurant ad in the yellow pages will say this. This is powerful and says that your restaurant must really be good.

5. Poor graphics and photos. Don't use fancy, hard to read type fonts or poor photos. Photographs can add to an ad, but they take up a lot of valuable space, so if you use a picture make sure it is top quality. Have a professional photographer make the photo and tell him or her that it will be used in a yellow page ad. By all means don't use a copy of a copy of any photo or graphics.

Don't have text on top of any background image. Graphic designers like to do this, but it makes your ad hard to read.

6. Your ad looks like all the other ads. Make your ad look like an article. Give it an editorial look with a headline and then text filled with benefits. Use subheads and bullet lists and make your ad informative and NOT dull. Most ads are boring and give no real reasons why anyone should eat at the restaurant.

Bonus technique

7. Most restaurant yellow page ads are too small. The six techniques described above will double or triple the response rate of your Yellow Page ad without you having to spend another dime.

Studies show that in most cases doubling the size of your yellow page ad will increase your response by over five times. (A quarter page ad will pull five times more response than an eighth page and a half page ad will pull five times more than a quarter page ad. And doubling the size of your ad will NOT double the cost of the ad.)

Invest in the largest yellow page ad you can afford. You usually pay for Yellow Page ads monthly at the end of the month AFTER the ad has brought you business all month. Since your larger ad will be bringing a lot of extra business, your new ad will be putting money in your bank account instead of taking money out of your pocket.

Also, consider spending extra money to have an ad with a white background instead of the conventional yellow background. Compare the price of this type of ad vs. a larger ad and see which one will give you more bang for the buck.

You want your ad to stand out and generally, having a white background on your ad will give better response than doubling the size of your ad. Of course, do both if your budget can handle it.

One last point: The bigger the ad, the better your restaurant is perceived to be and **"Perception IS reality."**

Bottom line: Take a look at your present yellow page ad and see how many of the above 7 mistakes are being made. Then find out when you have to have your new ad ready and don't cut it close. Start now and get your customer-grabbing Yellow Page ad ready. And invest in the largest Yellow Page ad you can afford.

By all means, don't let the ad salesperson write the ad for you and don't tell him or her to let the phone company's graphics department create the ad for you. If you do, your ad will look like all the other ineffective ads in the phone book. It will say, "Me, too," loud and clear.

## Chapter 7

Brochures and Fliers

How to design and use highly effective brochures and fliers

Most restaurant brochures and fliers fail to increase sales or profits and many of them would be considered a financial disaster if the real costs and results were tracked.

You can have one of the most highly effective brochures or fliers in the restaurant industry by avoiding the following seven common mistakes.

When you compare your brochures and fliers with these seven common mistakes, you will quickly see how they stack up and then it will be obvious to you how to turn your brochures and fliers into really powerful selling tools.

These are the seven most common mistakes made in restaurant brochures and fliers

1. Bad headline – or even worse, no headline

This is the biggest mistake of all. Nothing you can do to a brochure or a flier can overcome a bad headline. Do not use your company name or your logo as your headline. Your logo should be placed in the bottom left or right corner.

The most powerful headline you can have is one that answers the question, "What's in it for me?" Your headline should make a bold promise. Review the information in Chapter 4 about writing headlines.

Write at least a dozen headlines (two or three dozen would be better) before you settle on the best headline for your brochure.

Plan to spend more time writing and selecting the headline and sub-heads for your brochure or flier than you do for all of the other parts combined.

2. Dull or downright boring copy

Don't waste time telling how wonderful your company is and how long you have been in business. Fill the brochure with real benefits and not just facts and features. "We have a fireplace" is a feature. "Enjoy a quiet romantic dinner by the fire" is a benefit. When you list a feature, your customers will be saying to themselves, "So what?" Answer this question by telling the reader what's in it for him or her.

Put emotion into your brochure. Paint word pictures.

3. Haphazard and disorganized layout and flow

Your copy should flow in a way that will accomplish the "AIDA" format – **Attention, Interest, Desire** and finally **Action**. Use sub-heads also. If the readers looked at nothing except the headline and sub-heads, would they get the message and would it flow in the AIDA order?

4. Bad graphics

Having words printed over graphics or over a colored background (other than yellow) makes the text almost impossible to read. Your text should always be black type on a white background or on a yellow background. No exception. (Any shade of yellow from goldenrod to light yellow is fine.) You can use colors for headlines and sub-heads.

Use reverse type (white type on a black background) only for short headlines – **if** you use it at all. NEVER use it for the text. No one will read it.

Use serif typefaces (such as Times Roman) in the body copy. This makes it much easier to read. It's okay to use either serif or sans serif for the headlines and sub-heads. Don't use more than two typefaces.

Be sure to leave plenty of white space (or yellow space if you are using a yellow background).

5. No central theme

Your brochure or flier can't be all things to all people. You can't be telling about your romantic dinning atmosphere, your catering service and how wonderful your dining room is for weddings and special events all in the same brochure or flier. You can mention these other things in one catch-all sentence near the end, but you can't have the brochure or flier trying to emphasize all of these things. You should have a separate brochure for each one.

6. Wrong use of pictures

A picture can add a lot to a brochure, but it can also do more harm than good if it doesn't tie in with the headline and the general theme of the brochure. By all means include a caption under any picture you use. The caption should clearly state what's going on in the picture and **be sure to use a high quality photograph**. Hire a professional photographer if necessary, but don't use a dark or bad photo.

7. Call to action missing

Your brochure or flier should end with a strong call to action. What is it exactly that you want the reader to do? Call and book a reservation? Come in for your Tuesday night special? Book a Christmas party, birthday or anniversary celebration with you?

You have to make it crystal clear what it is you want the reader to do, such as this "**Call to Action:**"

```
        "Call 123-4567 right now and book your
reservations and mention this brochure for free
     appetizers for everyone in your party.
   This offer expires at the end of the month."
```

That's a strong call to action and an expiration date is always a good idea for any offer because it adds the urgency factor.

Of course, don't be strict on the expiration date. If someone comes in a little after the expiration date, honor the offer anyway and it will build a lot of good will. You can even tell the customer that the offer has expired, but since they are a new customer (or a regular customer) you are going to honor it. Make the customer feel special.

At the bottom of the brochure or flier be sure to include the name of your restaurant (you can also include your logo here). Also, include your address, phone number and hours of operation.

By all means, let people know where your restaurant is located. If it's not completely clear from your address, give a short description of where your restaurant is located. For example, say, "Across the street from Wal-Mart" or "Two blocks past the post office" or in the "Forest Lake Shopping Plaza."

If your restaurant is not near a recognizable landmark, then include a map in your brochure or flier. If you use a map, make it clear and easy to read. Most maps I've seen are totally useless – the print is so small and blurry it's impossible to read.

Two common types of brochure formats

The first option: Use standard 8½ x 11 paper tri-folded to form a 3 2/3 x 8½ inch brochure. (For a flier you can print two fliers on one 8½ x 11 sheet of paper and cut it in half.)

The second option: Use what is called a "rack card" format. This utilizes a heavier card stock that is 4 inches by 9 inches.

Unless you really have a **lot** to say and need both sides of an 8½ x 11 sheet of paper, go with the rack card design. You will need rack cards for hotel lobbies and other locations and you don't want to have to print two types of brochures.

Look on the Internet for "Brochure Printing" and you will find hundreds of sources. Look at several potential suppliers and order their free sample kits and check their prices. It's important that you actually see and feel the type of paper that will be used for your brochure. Coated stock provides a much better looking brochure.

Go by some local hotels and collect samples of the brochures in the card racks in their lobbies. See what type of brochures your competitors are using.

You should expect to pay from about 5 cents to 10 cents for each brochure depending on the type of paper and coating used and on the quantity ordered. I recommend that you order a minimum of 2,000 brochures and 5,000 to 10,000 or more would be an even better investment if you can afford it at all. Of course, be sure to have several people check over and proof the brochure before you commit to any quantity. If you are in a hurry to get brochures and are not sure that what you have is what you want to go with long term, it would be a good idea to start with 1,000 brochures mostly as a test.

To get a good deal on fliers, design and print a master and then have them copied for about 3 cents each. Most of the time fliers are used to promote special events, so you don't want to print large numbers. In most cases printing in color is not justified. You can produce attention-getting fliers, by printing them on white or any shade of yellow from goldenrod to light yellow paper. Do **not** print brochures on any color other than shades of yellow. Printing on colored paper other than yellow will be very hard to read. People won't read it. Be sure to get good ink coverage. You want your print to be very black. Many tests have proven that very black ink pulls almost two times more response than light or faded ink.

Two last points

#1. Be sure to include your company name, address, phone number, web address and hours of operation on all of your fliers and brochures. If your hours change with the seasons, you may want to leave the hours of operation off of your brochures because you will be printing a large number to last a long time. You don't want them to get out of date.

#2. When you're mailing out brochures, always include a sales letter with the brochure. If you are handing out fliers or brochures, they can stand alone.

Look over your brochures and fliers now and see how many of these seven mistakes are being made. Correct the mistakes and you could see a 2 to 10 times increase in the amount of business your brochures and fliers bring in – and making these changes will add absolutely zero extra cost.

Let's look at a real life example of how a flier was used.

An example of how to use fliers to quickly drive a starving crowd to your restaurant

Here are the details of a $96 technique Todd used shortly after he opened his new Pizza Bistro Restaurant . This technique really did create a crowd at his restaurant, he said, and **increased sales by over $1,000 a day.**

Todd's new Pizza Bistro had opened with reasonable success. He was doing better than break-even, which he thought was good for a new restaurant.

There had been a restaurant in the location before and a lot of traffic was passing his location every day. He had put up a new impressive looking sign a month before he opened announcing his grand opening day. Now he needed more business, and marketing money was almost non-existent.

Todd knew he had awesome pizza and wonderful Italian food. He also had fast delivery in his local area and a great atmosphere in his bar and dining room. How could he get this message to his potential customers and make them believe it? Here's how he got almost 100 extra customers a day starting before sundown the first day and with zero dollars to spend on advertising.

In his own words, here's Todd's story:

"It's simple. I sat down and wrote out what I had to offer on a half-sheet of paper. (I included a condensed menu printed on the back of the sheet.) I did the printing (two copies per page) on my back-office computer printer. I continued printing until I ran out of ink and had used up the spare ink cartridges I had.

Then I personally went to the five large apartment complexes in my area and stuck a sheet in every door. I didn't bother to ask the management office for permission, but I did deliver two free pizzas to each office and left some of the fliers. I never heard a complaint from anyone.

I spent zero dollars out of my pocket immediately, but I did calculate later that counting the ink and paper I had used up about $96 worth of supplies.

I got almost 100 new customers (including delivery orders) that first night after I distributed the fliers. New customers started coming in before sundown and they continued to come in the rest of the night. Handing out that one flier that one time continued to bring in business for a long time and got me a lot of regular customers.

What did I say in the flier? I wish I had kept a copy. One thing for sure was that I didn't cut any prices. I basically told them I had the best Italian food in town and that I would personally guarantee it.

I said to come in and ask for me (or call and place a delivery order) and if they didn't agree that I had the best Italian food and pizza in town, they wouldn't owe me a dime. On top of that, I would treat them to free bread sticks for the whole family.

I met a lot of wonderful people that night. I gave them special attention and invited them back as they were leaving. I think a lot of people kept coming in because they felt like they knew me. I tried to remember as many names (or at least, faces) as I could and I welcomed them back every time they came back in.

My sales were up over $1,000 a day for the next few days after I did this and I didn't do any additional advertising or marketing. My one-day marketing campaign gave me the boost I needed to get my new restaurant off and running.

Now I rely on an expanded version of this technique of distributing fliers in areas other than the apartment buildings."

"My plans are to start an email marketing campaign within a month. I have already started capturing people's names and email addresses in my data base."

Coupons are a special form of brochure or flier

Here's how to use coupons successfully

First, eliminate all strings in your special offers and watch your sales and profits skyrocket. Take the "**with**" and "**if**" terms out of your offers. Don't say, Free **with** the purchase of. . ." or "Free **if** you. . ." Most restaurant owners react in shock when I tell them this, but when they try it, they realize that it really does work wonders.

Next, realize that coupons for 10% off or even 20% off or buy one and get one free offers don't work. They are not perceived as anything special. I've heard people say, "Oh they probably jacked up the price 10% to cover the 10% off."

Coupons don't work if you offer them all the time or if you offer them for no special reason

Coupons can be a disaster of a short-term fix for a long-term problem.

Constantly offering discount coupons will train your customers to wait until they get another coupon in the mail or until they see one in the newspaper before they will come in to eat. These are not loyal customers; they are customers who look around every time they plan to eat out to see who is offering the biggest discounts.

Two things are important for every offer:

- **Tie the offer to a special occasion or to a "reason why"** – Free meal on your birthday or free meal because you are a Dr., attorney, CPA, firefighter, policeman, etc. There must be a reason why you're giving them a free meal.

- **Make the offer with absolutely no strings attached.**
  Don't say, "Free meal if there are three or more in the party or free entrée if you buy two drinks."

58

Restaurant marketing is not easy. That's the good news because when you start to implement the restaurant marketing techniques that work and eliminate the techniques that are a waste of money, your competition won't be able to hold a light to you.

You see a lot of advertisements that make promises so bold to get attention that they have to attach all kinds of stings to the offer in the fine print to be able to deliver. This leaves a bad taste in the readers' minds and doesn't leave the positive impression you want to create.

If you want to stand out, make offers that are totally free of strings. For example, say, "Come in on your birthday and your meal is totally free."

Yes, there will be a few (maybe 3%) who will come in by themselves, eat, not leave a tip and then leave to never be seen again – but the other 97% will bring people with them and likely come back again.

Even the people who don't come in for the offer will be far more likely to think highly of your restaurant and are likely to come in at a later time. They are also likely to tell their friends about your free offer and create a positive buzz about your restaurant.

Your competition will think you have lost your mind, but the restaurants that use this technique find that it's one of the most successful and least expensive marketing techniques in their marketing arsenal.

For example: Firehouse Subs does a massive mailing offering a free sub sandwich with no strings attached and every time they do this their sales shoot up and they pick up new loyal customers.

Give "no-strings attached" marketing a try and watch your business grow. You'll be pleasantly surprised how much profit it will generate and how few people take advantage of you.

How, When and IF to use coupons and discounts to promote your restaurant

Using coupons and discounts can bring in business, but what about profits? The use, or wrong use, of coupons and discounts can kill your restaurant profits – not just when you use them, but for months to come.

For example, when you go into a Sears store and go to their home appliance center, you will find at least one washer and dryer on sale, one or more models of refrigerators on sale, one model of dishwasher on sale, etc.

Who would pay top dollar and buy one of the other models that are not on sale? The units that are on sale are about the only ones that sell and the profit margins on these sale items are low.

Sears has tried several times to stop having these sales, but when they do, their sales drop drastically. Sears can say that they have stopped having sales (as they have done many times in the past), but no one believes them.

Every time they try this, they soon go back to having sales. They have trained their customers to expect sales. Their customers just wait them out.

Sears has hired Harvard marketing professors several times as consultants to analyze the problem and tell them how they can stop having sales.

I have talked to the Harvard professors Sears hired. They said they told Sears that the solution is simple – stop having sales and stay with it until your customers finally realize you mean it.

But every vice President of Marketing who tries it doesn't want to risk his or her job by watching sales go to pot while they wait it out. Therefore, they soon go back to business as usual.

The same is true with restaurants constantly using coupons. If they stop, sales will quickly drop. People only go out to eat occasionally and they don't always go to the same restaurant when they do go out.

If customers know they can find a coupon for your restaurant in the paper or in their mail or email every week or so, they will decide to wait and go to your restaurant when they get the next coupon. Tonight they will go somewhere else.

The constant use of coupons can get your customers hooked on them as sure as someone would get hooked on drugs. As Sears found out, when their customers do get hooked, it's very hard, if not almost impossible, to get them off the "coupon addiction " or "sale addiction."

So when should you use coupons and discounts?

Use coupons and discounts in the following cases ONLY!

- For special occasions like birthdays and anniversaries.

- For hotel and motel guests and convention and seminar attendees. You are only going to see these customers one time (or a few times at most), so you don't have to worry about getting them addicted to your coupons.

- For new people moving into town.

- You can also use coupons and discounts occasionally for situations like a grand opening, a totally new menu, celebrating your restaurant's anniversary date, introducing a new chef and maybe a few other situations. **The key is that the coupons and discounts have to be used rarely and ALWAYS for some special reason.**

When you do offer a discount, what offer works best?

Here is a quote from one restaurant owner, who tracks everything, –

> *"I have been tracking the results of my different flier promotions for the last two years now and by far the best offer is Free Appetizer with every entrée. We have used 20% off, Buy 1 get 1 Free, etc., but the best offer has definitely been the free appetizer."*

Your mileage may vary, but be sure to test to see which offer works best for you. It will depend on your menu and your customers. It may not be what you think, so be sure to track the response to different offers.

Bottom line: Coupons will always bring in extra sales and when sales are down, it's very tempting to use them. But it's the same as a drug addict deciding to use drugs when he is feeling, "down." Yes it may temporarily perk him up, but the results are short lived and it soon becomes an additive habit that's almost impossible to break – just ask Sears.

Use coupons and discounts responsibly and don't let your customers get hooked on them.

## Chapter 8

Email Marketing and Direct Mail Marketing

Introduction

The price of print and TV advertising has gone out of sight and the effectiveness is not what it used to be. An independent restaurant can go down the tube trying to compete with national chain restaurants using conventional advertising techniques.

To be really successful in the restaurant business today the use of email marketing and direct mail marketing are absolutely essential. We are going to start this chapter talking about email marketing and then near the end of the chapter we will cover the few additional things you need to know to add a direct mail campaign to your marketing program.

Email marketing can be extremely inexpensive (starting at $15 a month for a do it yourself solution).

In the first part of this chapter we will look at what solutions and programs are available for email marketing and compare the prices, features and benefits of two of the more popular programs. Then we will talk about how to implement the program you select.

Email Marketing

Let's start by selecting a software program and service provider.

Whatever you do, you don't want to send email messages from your own computer. It's a lot of work, not as many of your email messages will get through the filters and get opened and the most important reason not to do it is because you will certainly (because of being reported a few times for spam) have your email account canceled by your provider.

Here are some more of the reasons you don't want to send out email messages from your own computer. There are a lot of federal rules you have to follow when sending out bulk email messages and these rules change from time to time. Let someone else keep up with these rule changes. As an example, one of the rules states that you have to have a link in every email message that clearly allows the recipient to take their name off the list.

This feature needs to be built into the program that's being used to send out the email messages. All the email software and service providers I know of have this feature built into their software, but more than likely, the software on your own computer doesn't have this feature.

I can go on with the reasons not to do it, but just accept the fact that you don't want to send bulk email messages from your own computer.

Here's another thing to consider when selecting a software program and service provider.

There are basically two types of email messages – text messages (like the ones you get from your friends) and HTML type messages, which look like brochures or fliers, with color, pictures, large bold headlines, etc.

There's no doubt that HTML type email messages pull a two to three times greater response rate than text messages. The problem is that about 15% of email addresses are set to not see HTML messages. Many large companies and government agencies have their computers set so that employees don't see incoming HTML email messages. The reason for this is because it is more likely that a virus can be embedded in an HTML type email message than in a text type message.

Since HTML messages get a much larger response, but they don't all get seen, which way should you format your email messages?

Thanks to technology, there is a simple solution to this problem. You can send your email messages in a format called, **"Multi-**

part text/HTML MIME." This format sends the email in both formats and any email address set to not see the HTML email will automatically see the text message. It's heads you win and tails you don't lose.

The good news is that both of the programs I recommend below have this feature built in. Be sure any other software program and service you choose has this feature built in.

Now, let's get on with selecting the best email software and service provider for your restaurant.

There are over 250 email software and service provider programs on the market. You could almost throw a dart at the list and have a pretty good program. I don't know of any restaurant that can say their email-marketing endeavor wasn't successful because of the software program they were using.

I've looked at and evaluated about 10% of these 250 programs (selected based on personal experience and recommendations). I know you don't have time to evaluate 250 software programs – in fact, taking the time to evaluate 10% or 25 of these software solutions would probably not be the best use of your time.

Below are the pros and cons of two different programs I think you should consider. Both of these recommended programs fill a different need. No one program is the best for every restaurant.

This is not to say that there are not other programs out there that could do just as good of a job for you and maybe even better, but you can't go wrong if you select one of the two programs below. In addition to my comments, be sure to go to the actual websites and look at the descriptions and the pros and cons of each program and evaluate how suitable it is for your restaurant.

In fact, since both programs have a free trial available, if you have the time, it would be a good idea to sign up for the free trial for both programs, enter half a dozen email addresses (yours and some friends or employees), send out a couple of emails and see how comfortable you feel with the program.

Let's look at the two programs I think would do a good job for you:

www.FishBowl.com is a complete software solution to basically do **everything** for you. They furnish the preprinted sign-up forms along with pre-addressed and postage-paid envelopes for you to mail in the filled out forms each week.

They actually do the data entry for you and send out great looking brochure type email messages. There is no effort on your part except to get your staff to ask the guests to fill out the forms to get on your birthday list.

FishBowl specializes in email marketing for restaurants only, so you can imagine that they have some very effective and convincing emails already designed and ready for restaurant owners and managers to send out.

Over 14,000 restaurants use their service including a lot of big name chain restaurants. This tells me their service is effective and is generating a profit for their customers.

This is a good solution for restaurants that are never going to get around to setting up their own program. It takes almost no effort from the restaurant owner or manager other than writing a $200 monthly check and making sure servers are getting the forms filled out.

The $200 a month they charge includes everything – furnishing the sign up forms, doing the data entry and sending out great looking emails for birthdays, anniversaries, welcoming first time guests and as many special occasions as you select. Yes, you can send out as many email messages as you want to and you can send them to as many email addresses as you want. The $200 a month covers it all.

The cons or disadvantages of the FishBowl program are the cost and the fact that you can't collect any information other than their standard, name, email address, birthday and wedding anniversary. You don't get to capture the guests' physical addresses, or how they heard about your restaurant or what they thought about your food and service. With a physical address, you can get an idea where your customers are coming from (how far away) and you can also mail out letters and brochures (which we talked about in the previous chapter).

Of course, when you have a customer's email address, you can always send them an email asking for their physical address and asking how they liked the food and service.

Another option for getting this extra data is to capture it on a separate form and enter it into your own Excel database. This is easy to set up and you can use a mail merge program to personalize letters and post cards to send out later when you get around to it.

Bottom line: FishBowl is a great service for restaurant owners and managers who don't have the time or expertise to do the data entry and implement a more complete data collection technique. It's more expensive than the next service I will talk about, but it sure beats not doing anything and it takes almost no time or effort from management.

The next service to consider is **www.ConstantContact.com**. One of the best features of this program is its simplicity and user friendliness. It also comes with a manual, instructional video and great free customer support from 9:00 A.M.. until 9:00 P.M. Eastern time. It's very easy for you to get up and running with this program.

Constant Contact has about 140 pre-designed templates – many of them designed especially for restaurants. Of course, you can design your own templates for any special mailings you want to do.

They also allow up to 15 special fields that you can customize and set up to capture information other than the basic information. You can capture physical addresses, where they heard about your restaurant, how they liked your food and service, etc.

The cost of Constant Contact's service is very reasonable at $15/mo. for up to 500 email addresses, $30/mo. for up to 2,500 email addresses, $50/mo. for up 5,000 names and $75/mo. for up to 10,000 email addresses.

Constant Contact also has a survey option you can add later for a few more dollars a month. This can be a great way to get ideas and opinions from your customers.

Bottom line: The Constant Contact program is being used by, and was recommended by, more people in a recent survey than any other program I evaluated – and with good reason. It's inexpensive and you can be up and running with this program almost immediately.

Be sure to think about your needs and the staff you have available to set up and implement a system when selecting a program. Take the time to go to the two websites listed above and see for yourself just what they have to offer, how each one fits with your needs and which one you feel comfortable with.

If you go with Constant Contact, you will need to create and print your own data collection forms to capture the information about your customers. Below is an example of an Excel document that I created in a matter of minutes. Feel free to create your own form using this format. You may want more or fewer data fields. I recommend that you ask for all of the information on the form. It will prove valuable in your marketing efforts. You could just capture the name, birthday and email address, but I like to get more information. Asking for more information doesn't seem to reduce the number of forms you're able to collect.

If you don't know how or don't have the time to create the form in Excel or another program, I'm sure there are people on your staff who are experts in Excel. Almost all students have had to do a lot of Excel projects in school. There's a sample form to get you started on the next page

You can put your logo or other information in the section at the top. The box will not normally be there when you design your form. I just wanted to make sure you saw it.

Restaurant Name	
Please join our Birthday Club. **Privacy Policy:** We totally respect your privacy. We never sell or share this information with anyone. It is used for our in-house marketing only to send you discount offers and birthday wishes. Please omit any information you don't wish to share. Thank you. **Please Print.**	Your Logo Here
Last Name	
First Name	
Circle One	Mr. Ms.
E-Mail Address	
Mailing Address	
Apt. #	
City	
ST	
Zip Code	
Phone #	
Circle One	Home Cell Business
Birthday	(month & day)
Spouse's First Name	
Spouse's Birthday	(month & day)
Is this your 1st visit?	Yes No
How did you hear about us or why did you sellect us for this visit?	
How was your food? 1=bad & 5=excellent	Circle one 1 2 3 4 5
How was the service? 1=bad & 5=exellent	Circle one 1 2 3 4 5
Your Server's Name	
Any other comments are welcome. Thanks for joining our Birthday Club.	

One last point: you can't honestly say that money is so tight right now that you can't afford to implement an email marketing program, because you can sign up for the free trial for either service and the extra profit generated during the month will more than pay the fee at the end of the month to continue the service. If it doesn't generate this much extra income, you shouldn't be doing email marketing anyway – but I've never seen a restaurant email marketing program that didn't work – that is, **if** the names were actually collected.

How to collect names and email addresses – Use contests and teams

The biggest problem with any email-marketing program is that it never gets fully implemented. If management is not 100% behind it, it will never get off the ground. At every employee meeting you need to talk about how many names were collected last week.

I've seen it happen over and over again, a restaurant implements an email-marketing program with great fan-fare and the servers start collecting names, but then the first thing you know, no one is collecting names anymore.

The three best ways to make sure the enthusiasm for collecting the names doesn't fizzle out are as follows:

1. Management has to make it known that the project is important to them and let it be known that the data are being tracked. As I said before, referring to the number of names collected at every employee meeting is a great way to get the point across.

2. Have contests every week or every month. If the servers are not working approximately an equal number of hours a week, consider rewarding the person who collected the most number of names per hour worked. Maybe also recognize the person who collected the most total names as well. Give away something of value to the winners – two tickets to the movies or a bottle of good wine (if they are over 21) or a free dinner for two. Many restaurants have found that their suppliers or local businesses will provide the prizes. This way there is no cost to you.

3. The third technique is the one I really like and I have found to work great. The technique is to divide the staff up into teams. Pare a dishwasher, bus person, cook, etc. with a server. This way everyone gets to participate in the contest and believe me, the person back in the kitchen will be constantly asking their server partner, "How many cards did WE get tonight?" It keeps the servers on their toes and it builds camaraderie among your staff. You might even want to change the paring from time to time, so that a bus person doesn't get stuck with a server who is never going to work hard enough at collecting names to win.

Making your program work – What to send and how often

Even though both of the programs described allow you to send out an unlimited number of email messages, you don't want to overdo it. You have permission from your customers to send them email messages, but I doubt if they want to be constantly bombarded.

In most cases, one or two messages a month would be about right – one a week at the most.

This was said before, but it bears repeating. Claude Hopkins, one of the greatest marketing gurus of all times said, **"Don't advertise unless you have news of value"**. You don't want your email messages to be saying basically, "It's me again. Don't forget about me." Make sure that every email message you send out has some "news of value" for your customer.

That doesn't mean that you have to constantly send out discount offers. In fact, as described previously, this can backfire and your customers may start waiting for a discount coupon before they visit your restaurant.

You can tell them that you now have live entertainment on Friday and Saturday nights, or that you have just added North Atlantic Salmon to the menu or that you have added your grandmother's recipe for blackberry cobbler to the menu. You get the idea.

One very important point is to **never** refer to your customer or guest as a customer or guest. **Always** use the word, "you." And by all means, never say anything like, "We wanted to let everyone know blah, blah, etc." Write the email as if you were talking to **one** person only. Say, "I want to let you know blah, blah, etc."

Both of the email services we talked about previously usually word the emails in their templates correctly, but be sure to double check before you okay a message to be sent out.

Direct Mail Marketing

Direct mail marketing is closely tied to email marketing. The good part is that there is not too much new stuff you have to learn after you have learned how to do email marketing. The use of headlines, collecting names, how to make offers and write ad copy are all the same. The only thing that's different is the mechanics of how you actually implement your direct mail marketing program.

Of course, direct mail marketing is a lot more trouble and a lot more expensive than email marketing, so why would any restaurant choose to do it? There is only one reason – it pays off.

A letter in an envelope or a post card will always get a much higher response than an email message, but of course, it costs more and is a lot more trouble. But when done right, the return on your investment for a direct mail marketing campaign can greatly outweigh the cost and prove to be very profitable.

The best way to test direct mail marketing is on a limited basis and for special occasions. The very best response to direct mail marketing will be for birthdays. Yes, you will get a good response with your email marketing for birthdays, but you will get a much better response by actually sending out a letter or card.

The problem with an email message is that a high percentage of email messages will never get opened. Of course, this can be a problem with a direct mail letter, too—especially if it looks like junk mail.

My advice is to do mostly email marketing, but mix in a few direct mail letters (or post cards) and be sure to track the results closely. Since the physical addresses are already in your database and by using a mail merge program in MS Word or another program, the actual effort to get the letters out can be minimal.

Here are the rules and steps to follow to make a direct mail marketing program successful:

1. Do **not** use bulk mail (except for your newsletter which is clearly marked as your newsletter on the envelope). Place a real live first class stamp on the envelope. Bulk mail looks like junk mail – because it usually is.

2. Use plain white envelopes. For a little extra expense, you can have the envelopes preprinted with a message or buy a rubber stamp and add a message on the outside of the envelope that will help get the letters opened. Words like, "Happy Birthday" or "Here's the information you requested." (Actually they did request that you send them information. That's why they signed up to be on your mailing list.)

3. Hand addressing the envelopes will greatly increase the response rate because the letter will be sure to be opened, but this may add way too much cost. Consider it and decide.

4. The rules for fliers and brochures apply to writing direct mail pieces – no colored paper (except shades of yellow), the headline is the most important part of the letter, etc. One rule especially for letters is to **always add a P.S.** The headline and P.S. will be read even if nothing else in the letter gets read.

5. Be sure to sign each letter by hand in bright blue ink. Don't use a dark blue that looks almost black. Using a felt tip pen works good. You want it to be obvious that the letter was signed by a real person and that it is not a computer generated signature.

6. Fold the letters in a "Z" fold so the headline is clearly visible as soon as the letter is taken out of the envelope.

7. Be sure to collect the letters that are returned and not delivered and take these addresses out of your database. You don't want to keep wasting postage on letters that are not going to be delivered. I would suggest that you send an email or call the person and see if you can get a correct address. Maybe it was a problem reading someone's handwriting when the address was entered into your data bank or maybe they have moved. Even if they have moved, their email address will probably still be the same and they may have just moved somewhere that is still within your marketing area. This is one of your valued customers. Don't give up on them without one final effort to get a good address.

8. Just like fliers, be sure to write the letter to only **one** person. Don't say, "I am sending this to our best customers." Instead say, "Joe, I wanted to invite you to. . . " With mail merge programs it's easy to send the letter to "Dear Joe" instead of "Dear Friend" and it will be worth the small effort involved.

There is one special kind of direct mail marketing that works better than all the others combined – it's a Newsletter!

How to create a customer newsletter and make it your most cost-effective marketing tool

Nothing does more to create customer loyalty than your own newsletter. Here are the templates, topics, sub-heads, layout techniques and everything you need to quickly, easily and inexpensively publish your own newsletter.

Topics to cover in your newsletter

Below is a list of topics you can consider covering in your newsletter. Some of these you may want to have as a regular section every month and some could be used occasionally.

- Feature article

- News from the chef
- New menu items
- Editor's notes
- Guest article
- **Quote of the month** – Mark Twain is a good source for quotes.
- Joke for the month
- Music schedule
- Readers feedback and comments
- **Upcoming events** – Homecoming weekend at the local college, Bike Week, the local Rose Festival – anything that's big in the community.
- **Recipes** – they don't have to be recipes for items on your menu.
- **Funny stories about your restaurant or guests** – a guest drove off and forgot his wife, etc.
- **Announcements** – such as, "Mr. and Mrs. John Jones celebrated their 25th anniversary with us on February 12th.

Mechanics of your newsletter

There is no one right way to produce your newsletter, but there are a lot of wrong ways to do it.

Here are the points you should keep in mind so you will avoid the wrong ways to do it:

- When you begin, keep it to one page front and back. Later you can go to a 11" x 17" sheet which will fold to be two standard size sheets in a book format. This will give you four pages for content.
- Write your newsletters like you were writing to only one person. Picture a customer in your mind and write the

newsletter to just that one person. It will be easier to write and it will sound much more personal – which is what you want to accomplish.

- Mail it once a month and try to mail it on the same day every month.

- Send your finished newsletter to a print shop and have them do the actual printing. Be sure to have your print shop print some extra copies so you can give them out at your restaurant to customers who are not on your mailing list.

- Use a mailing house to do the actual stuffing and mailing and use their bulk mail permit. They are set up to do all the work automatically including stuffing and addressing the envelopes and printing their bulk mail postage on the envelopes. They can do it at a much lower cost than you can. Shop around for the best price.

- Until you get the hang of it, don't date your newsletters. Maybe say October, 2009, etc., but don't put an actual date on it because you may run late some months in the beginning. (Keep in mind that bulk mail doesn't get delivered as quickly as first class mail.) Be sure your name is on the mailing list so you will receive a copy of the newsletter. This way you will know when it actually gets delivered.

- Do your birthday mailings (and any other direct mail promotion) by first class mail instead of using bulk mail. With first class mail you will get returns for the bad addresses for the people who have moved, etc. This will clean your list once a year so you don't continue to pay to mail newsletters that are not getting delivered.

- Whether you are using an envelope or putting the address on the outside of the folded newsletter, be sure to have a section with large print in the area to the left of where the address will go and have the print say, "**Here's your Newsletter**" or something similar to that. Also, print it at an angle so it will stand out. Your newsletter will be perceived as being of higher quality if you send it in an envelope, but some restaurants elect to save money and print the address on the folded newsletter. This works better on the 11" x 17" size newsletter than it does on the single sheet newsletter.

- If you don't like to write, have someone on your staff write the newsletter, but it is better if you actually write it. Maybe have someone write the basic newsletter every month and you only write one section like the "Editor's Notes." Regardless of who writes it, have **two** people proof the newsletter before it goes to the printer. When changes are made have them proof it again.

- Keep your newsletter personal. If your dog dies, or your daughter gets married, or you have a new grand-baby or you have been on a vacation, talk about it.

- Design your newsletter so it can be scanned. Most people will not read it word-for-word and will scan it at first and then maybe just read the sections that interest them. Use sub-heads and bullets a lot.

- Always print black on white. You can have color around the edge, but **never** print text on a colored background (other than some shade of yellow) because it is very hard to read and people will **not** read it. The only exception is that you can have a few large words printed on color in a heading.

- Be sure to end each newsletter with a script signature. Make it very legible (regardless of what your regular signature looks like.) Follow the signature with text of your name and title (John Jones, owner or Jenny Johnson, General Manager, etc.)

- If you're using any shade of blue on your newsletter, have your signature in blue also. This makes it look like it was actually signed by you instead of by a computer.

- One way to have a color newsletter at a low-cost is to design a sheet with your logo or heading and maybe a few lines of color to mark off sections, etc., then print a large quantity of these sheets. Then give them to your printer to print the black text on each month. The back side can always be black text and no color. Color printing is not expensive when printing large quantities, but it gets expensive for short runs.

- Don't be tempted to offer specials or discount coupons as part of your newsletter. You don't want to train your customers to wait for the newsletter coupon before coming to your restaurant.

- Consider using season related contests to create interest. Next month you can report on the winners. This gives you more to write about. Contests such as guessing how many black seeds are in a watermelon might be an interesting contest near the 4th of July.

- **Do NOT send your newsletter by email**. Mail your newsletter and if you have more than a few hundred names and addresses, use a mailing service and use their bulk mail permit.

- To stay in contact with your customers, I suggest that you mail your newsletter once a month and also send out **two** email messages a month.

- At the bottom of the front page be sure to include your website, physical address and phone number. Also, tell people how to sign up for your birthday list and get a free dinner on their birthday and receive your newsletter. Your customers will be passing your newsletter along to friends.

- Some sample newsletter templates are shown below. Color looks professional and gets more attention, but it's more expensive. You can have a great looking newsletter using some of the templates shown below that are only black and white.

Below is a link to some Microsoft Office templates. Don't worry that a lot of the sample templates say that they are for real estate newsletters. They can work just as well for a restaurant.

office.microsoft.com/en-us/templates/CT101043281033.aspx?av=ZPB000

Here is a link to a simple two page black and white newsletter template that is very popular.

tinyurl.com/n6ngc2

Or you can just type in:

www.Office.Microsoft.com/templates

Then you can start clicking on links until you find the templates you like.

You can use Microsoft Office to design a custom newsletter template, but your format is not nearly as important as most people think. Don't go overboard and try to make it too fancy. Don't let some graphics designer go wild.

Of course, all of this depends on your having a list of physical addresses of your customers. If you don't have a list or have not been capturing physical addresses, then you should start immediately. For most restaurants I recommend **www.ConstantContact.com** to do your emails. They will keep your database of physical addresses, also. You can put a link on your website so people can go to their site and get on your mailing list and email list.

Start your newsletter and get one out by next month. Do this even if you have not captured a single customer's name and address yet. Start capturing names now and you can have 100 or so by the time you get your newsletter written.

Starting small is a great way to launch your newsletter. With a small number you can print them on your printer and have someone on your staff stuff the envelopes. You can use mail merge to address the envelopes.

Your first newsletters can even be on one side of one sheet of paper. You can add more content and make a larger newsletter later.

## Chapter 9

Internet Marketing

Internet marketing is one of the best and most profitable marketing opportunities in the history of the restaurant industry and it's getting more popular and profitable all the time. If email marketing was counted in with Internet marketing, then Internet marketing would be better than all other kinds of marketing combined.

 In the Bed and Breakfast industry, Internet marketing has just about totally replaced all other forms of advertising. The old printed directories are becoming a thing of the past. Is the marketing for restaurants going to be the next industry to be taken over by the Internet? Probably not for a while yet, but the Internet is getting to be very effective for the restaurants that are taking advantage of it.

The good news for you is that not many restaurant owners are making full use of the Internet to market their restaurants. In fact, most of them are not using it at all. Also, a lot of restaurant owners who think they're using the Internet are really not because their websites are buried so far down in the indexes of Google and the other search engine that they will never see the light of day. And if someone did stumble across their websites, there is nothing on the websites to convince anyone to visit the restaurants. All of this is good news for you.

The Internet is growing by leaps and bounds. By some estimates the percentage of people who search the Internet before they go out to eat is doubling every year. You don't want to miss out on this market any longer.

If you already have a website, the following section will show you how to see if it was designed correctly or if it is a total disaster. How fancy and pretty the website looks is not what's important to making money on the Internet. Below is what's important. (**And if you don't have a website yet**, keep reading and I will show you how to have one before sundown.)

It is not my intention of this next section to teach you how to design a complicated web page. But **it is the purpose of this section to show you how to quickly tell if your website is designed correctly and show you how you can have basic website quick and easy.**

A lot of website designers are great graphic designers and can create stunning websites, but in many cases the way they design websites almost ensures that Google and the other search engines will never consider their website designs to be worthy of being ranked near the top

When it comes to your website, you shouldn't rely on what anyone tells you when it's so easy to check and see for yourself.

Here are the few things you need to know that will quickly make you an expert at analyzing websites and allow you to easily check out your own website to see if it's designed correctly.

Go to your website Home page and hit Ctrl+U (hold down the Control key and hit the "U" key – upper or lower case doesn't matter) and the source code for your Home web page will pop up on the screen. Don't be intimidated by what might look like Greek or hieroglyphics to you. Don't worry. There are only a few things on the page you need to look at.

Note: (The "Control U" function is the same as going to the top menu and clicking "View" and then clicking on "Page Source" in the drop-down menu. These instructions are for a PC. If you have a Mac, you have to do it a little differently. You click on "View" at the top of the page and then in the drop-down menu click on "Page Source" or use "Command+U" for a shortcut.)

Scroll down the page a little until you see the word, "HEAD" surrounded by brackets as shown below:

<HEAD>

A few lines of code below the <HEAD> comment you will probably see the following three lines of code (not necessarily in the order shown and all three lines might not even be there). There may be some other code mixed in between the lines, but all you are looking for are the following three lines of code. You will find these before you get down to the end of the HEAD section which will be marked by the HEAD with a backslash in front of it like this: </HEAD>

Here are the three lines of code that are important. (Later, you might even want to check out your competitors' websites and see if their websites are designed correctly.) Here are the three lines of code.

<META NAME="Description" CONTENT="Some text will show up here, hopefully describing your website">

<META NAME="Keywords" CONTENT="A list of your important keywords and keyword phrases will be here">

<TITLE>The title of your website will be here. It should be 10 to 15 words long and include your most important keywords and keyword phrases near the beginning. </TITLE>

</HEAD> (This signals the end of the HEAD section. The above three lines of code will show up before you get to his line of code.)

Here are the things to look for in these three lines of code.

Let's start at the bottom of the list with the TITLE. This is the most important part of your website. This is the Title of your website. It is **not** the same as the headline that shows up on your web page.

In order to rank high on Google or the other search engines, the keywords and keyword phrases that you want to rank high for almost have to be included in the Title tag of your website.

Google looks at only the first 83 characters and spaces of the TITLE, so your keywords must be included in about 10 to 15 words depending on how big the words are. Also, the first words in the Title are considered the most important. So it is very important that your most important keyword phrase be the first words in your TITLE. You don't want to waste the space in your TITLE with words that no one is going to search for. For example, you probably don't want to include the name of your restaurant because you will rank high for the name of your restaurant anyway.

Here are some sample Titles formats that you might want to copy:

<Title>Seafood Restaurant Charleston, SC South Carolina downtown historic district restaurants</Title>

(Include the keywords you think your potential customers are most likely to be searching for and don't waste the valuable few words you have by including words that will not be used in a search.)

If your keywords are in the name of your restaurant and the name of your restaurant is short, you can use it in your Title like the example shown below:

<TITLE>Jack's seafood and steakhouse restaurant Savannah GA Georgia water view waterfront restaurants</TITLE>

Note that the abbreviation and the full name of the state are included in both examples because people might enter it either way in their search. Also, note the insertion of the important words, "water view" and "waterfront" in the second example and the use of both the singular and plural versions of the word, "restaurant."

By all means, don't waste any of the few words in your Title tag by including your domain name or URL. In other words, don't include www.JacksSeafoodRestaurant.com in your Title tag. If someone searches for your domain name, your restaurant will be found anyway.

If you see your domain name in your Title tag, you will know that your web designer didn't do a good job of optimizing your website. And if your domain name is the only text included in your Title tag, you will know that he did a very bad job of designing your website. The designer you used may be a great graphics designer, but you don't want him/her doing anymore work on your website.

The next thing to look at is the Description Tag. This will not help your search engine rankings, but most of the time Google will use the text in the Description Tag as the description they show when your website shows up in their search results.

The Description Tag should be considered as an ad for your website. When someone sees your website on the list of sites that show up in the search engine results pages called SERP, hopefully the Description Tag shown will convince them to click on the link to your website. The Description doesn't have to be correct according to grammar rules, but it does need to make sense and read smoothly.

Sometimes websites don't even have a Description Tag – another sign of an incompetent website designer.

The third thing you need to look at is the Keyword Tag. The words in Keyword Tag are not seen by any of the search engines except Yahoo and even Yahoo doesn't count them very much at all towards your ranking.

You can only effectively optimize a web page for two to three keywords (five at the absolute max.). So, when you see a dozen or more keywords listed like it was a wish list, you know that your website designer doesn't have a clue what he's doing.

The only real use for the Keyword Tag is so you can remember which keywords you are trying to optimize the page for. Every web page should have a different Title and be optimized for a different set of two to five keyword phrases.

Looking at these three lines of code will tell you quickly if your website designer knows what he's doing or not.

Here are a few more things you can do. The actual headline that viewers see when they go to your website should show up on this page of code enclosed inside H1 code like this: It will be a lot further down the page.

<H1>The headline on your website</H1>

Then your subheads or headlines used for paragraph headings on the page should look like this:

<H2>The text for your subheads should show up here</H2>

And even smaller subheads could use H3 code.

There should only be one H1 headline on the page and there can be several H2 and H3 subheads.

Sometimes website designers use what is called JavaScript™ to code the headlines and you will not see them as described above. If you don't see the headlines on this Source code page, the search engines won't see them and your site will never rank high for these keywords. It is very important for your website to have your most important keywords in your headline and in your subheads and that these headlines and subheads show up in H1 and H2 code.

This point bears repeating. Just because you see your headline on your webpage doesn't mean that the search engines see it. If you don't see your headline in the H1 code as described above, then the search engines are not going to see it. Putting headlines in JavaScript™ will make them show up on the web page, but the search engines won't see them.

When you are talking to a website designer, here is one sure way to know that they are trying to take advantage of you. If they say that they will submit your website to hundreds of search engines, you know immediately that either they think you aren't knowledgeable about websites and they can charge you big bucks or else they are totally ignorant about how search engines work.

There are two main reasons why promising to submit your website to hundreds of search engines is a BS statement. . .

#1. There are only four search engines that matter. They have 99% of the search engine traffic. Google gets about 64%, Yahoo gets 22%, MSN gets 9% and Ask gets 4%. That leaves 1% for the hundreds of other search engines.

#2. The second reason is that even if you submitted a site to Google or the other search engines, they wouldn't index your site unless there are some other sites linking to it and if there are other sites linking to your site, Google and the other search engines will find your site anyway. It's like in the restaurant business. People don't want to stop at a restaurant if there are no other cars in the parking lot. Likewise, Google and the other search engines don't want to put a website in their index if no one else thinks it's important enough to link to. (We will talk about links later in the chapter.)

So if a website designer ever says, "I will submit your website to hundreds of other websites," he is either trying to rip you off or he is dumb as an ox about how to design websites. Either way, you don't want him anywhere near your website.

There is an old joke with a lot of truth in it that says, "The difference between a used car salesman and a website designer is that a used car salesman knows when he's lying."

For any website designer you are considering hiring, be sure to look at two or three of the websites he has designed and check the factors discussed above. Forget about how great the sites look. If he doesn't know how to get the basics right, you can be sure that there are 101 other things about website design that he doesn't know either. Bottom line: You don't want him designing your website. Let him go work on your competitors' websites.

But look on the bright side, after you check all the factors discussed above, you may find that your website is designed correctly.

I suggest you go back and read this section again. It's not really as complicated as it sounds and the knowledge could save you thousands of dollars. Knowing these basic things about website design can keep you from paying (or continuing to pay) a website designer who doesn't have a clue what he's doing. Not only are you paying him a lot of money, is he costing you money by preventing your website from ever ranking high in the search engines.

Now that you know the above facts, you know more than 99.9% of restaurant owners about whether a website is designed properly or not and, I'm sorry to say, you know more than a lot of website designers. With your new knowledge, you can use the Internet to fill your restaurant.

Below is more information on the factors we have been discussing and a few more factors that are important to search engines. You don't have to know all of this, but you can make more money from your website if you do.

How to tweak the 7 on-page factors that really matter to search engines

I watch search engines like a hawk and constantly run tests and track results to learn what works and what doesn't. Here's what works.

To rank high over the long haul and to get a lot of business from your website, you have to create a web page that will give searchers what they want. The search engines will reward you for this. Google and the other search engines want to make their customers happy and keep them coming back. The only way they can do this is by giving searchers what they want.

When searchers constantly find what they're looking for by using a certain search engine, they will continue to use that search engine. This way the search engine gets more users and can sell more ads and charge more for their ads. After all, Google and the other search engines are in business to make money. Your job is to help them do this by providing great Web sites. Note: Some of these things we have gone over before, but let's go over them again and in a little more detail.

How to tweak the 7 most important on-page factors for high search engine rankings

- **Title:** Not having a proper Title tag hurts more websites than anything I come across. Writing a good Title is simple. (Keep in mind that the Title of your website and the headline that shows on your Web page are **not** the same thing.) Put your most important keyword phrase at the beginning of the Title and use the words in the order most likely to be searched for. Repeat your keyword in different variations (plural, etc.) when applicable or use it again in a different phrase, but only repeat it **one** time. Google will see the first 83 characters and spaces, so use 10 to 15 words. Have a different Title for each page. That's all there is to it. Don't put your restaurant name in your Title tag unless it is short and descriptive. Your site is going to rank high for your restaurant name anyway. It's usually a good idea to include your state spelled out and use the abbreviation. Include the name of the city and also include the word "restaurant" and the word "restaurants" since people search using both these different phrases.

- **Meta tags:** The Description tag is the only Meta tag that's important and it's only important because it's used to describe your page in the search engine results – **not** because it will have anything at all to do with boosting your search engine rankings. When it comes to the Keyword META tag, it is only looked at by Yahoo and they don't value it much. The only real purpose for it is to help you remember which keywords you are optimizing the page for. You will see a lot of websites that use the Keyword Meta Tag as a wish list for all of the words and phrases they wish they could rank high for. This is a sign of a website designed by someone who doesn't know what he's doing. If you're paying someone to design and support your website and he does this, you know you are wasting your money.

- **Keywords in the text:** Everyone wants to know, what is the magic number for keyword density? (Keyword density is the total number of times a keyword is used on a page divided by the total number of words on the page.) The truth is, "There ain't no magic number for keyword density." Make your text read natural. If you have to have a number, 0.5% to 2% is good. Never more than 5%. A keyword density of 10% to even 20% used to get you to the top. Now those numbers will be considered spam and may even get your website banned. What is important about keywords is to use them in your headline and subheads and use them in bold and/or italics at least one time, but **never** put a keyword in bold or italics the first time you use it on the page. The most important thing (to Google and to your readers) is that your text reads naturally and it doesn't sound like it has been stuffed with keywords.

- **Keywords in the headlines and subheads:** Use the H1 header for your first headline and include your most important keyword phrase in the headline. Then use keyword-rich H2 headers for paragraph headlines. These are usually referred to as subheads.

- **Number of words on the page:** The length of a page should be like a woman's skirt – long enough to cover the subject and short enough to be interesting. About 250 to 1,000 words is a good range. I see a lot of Web pages with several pictures and almost no words. There may be words that are visible on the Web page, but they are in JavaScript™ and you will not see them on the page when you hit Ctrl+U and Google and the other search engines won't see them either. Google likes **words** that they can see. Some graphic designers like to use JavaScript™, but this could kill an otherwise good website.

- **Age of the page:** It was revealed in the Google patent application that Google considered the age of a page (as determined by the first time they indexed the page) as a very important factor in search engine page rank – probably because this is one factor that can't be manipulated. Of course, there is nothing you can do about this, but think about it if you are considering changing the domain name of your website. It might be better to keep what you have unless it is really bad.

- **Links:** Incoming links are king when it comes to getting high rankings, but out-going links on the page can have some effect also. Be sure to link to a few on-topic web pages from your site. But the one factor that counts more than anything else towards high ranking is the number and authority of other sites that are linking to your site. The search engines consider that if another site thinks your site is good enough for them to link to, it must be pretty good and the more sites that link to your site the more important your site must be. A link from a high ranking site is more valuable than a link from a low ranking site and an on-topic link is more valuable than an off-topic link. For example, if you have a BBQ restaurant, a link from another BBQ restaurant site would be more valuable than a link from a dress shop.

No one element of a page is going to make it rank high, but doing a lot of little things right will make the difference between being on page 10 and on page ONE.

Tight horse races are won by a nose. The winning horse is not 10 times faster than the horse that came in 10th and the #1 ranked web site is not 10 times better than the #10 ranked site. So go tweak the little things on your site and watch your rankings climb.

How to find the best keywords and keyword phrases for your website

When people search the Internet, you want them to find your website. To do this your site has to be ranked high for the words and phrases they search for. For example, if someone searched for "Seafood restaurant Denver" or "Seafood restaurants in Denver" and you had a seafood restaurant in Denver, you would want them to find your restaurant.

To make this happen, your restaurant website would have to be optimized for the phrase that was searched for. Notice in the example above that one of the searches used the term, *restaurant* and one used the word, *restaurants*. Since people do this, you would want to use both the singular and the plural versions in your Title tag and on your Web page. These words would be what are called "Keywords."

The key to ranking high is try to decide which phrases people will most likely be searching for and then have your website optimized for those phrases. By optimized, I mean use the words in your Title tag, in the headline on your page and in the subheads. Use the words in bold and in italics in the text on the page a time or two, but not the first time the word is used on the page.

If you want some help in finding out which phrases people search for the most, use one of the tools below:

Google's Keyword Tool **is** free and Wordtracker will cost you about $60 for a one month subscription (except sometimes they offer a 7-day free trial). You will get a lot more information from the Wordtracker site, but the Google Keyword Tool is easier to use an it's free. Use these tools to help you come up with keywords you had not thought of and to help to tell you which keywords are searched for the most often.

Google Keyword Tool.

https://adwords.google.com/select/KeywordToolExternal

The Google Keyword Tool will show you what people are actually searching for, the number of competitors, and the monthly search volume for each of those words.

"To see how valuable Google's new Keyword Tool can be to you, consider the two phrases, "discount weddings" and "cheap wedding.""

To me they mean the same thing and I would expect them to get about the same number of searches, but "discount weddings" gets about 1,000 searches a month and "cheap wedding" gets 246,000 searches.

WOW, what a difference. So if you are going after the wedding reception catering business, this tells you that optimizing your website for the phrase *cheap wedding* is a phrase that you would want to consider optimizing for.

Using the Google Keyword Tool, you can get keyword and phrase suggestions from Google based on actual search history by Google users, as related to the content of your web site or the text of your Google AdWords ads.

The Google Keywords Tool will show you what people are actually searching for, the number of competitors and the monthly search volume for each of those words.

Wordtracker

www.Wordtracker.com

Wordtracker usually charges about $60 for a one-month subscription, but from time to time they offer a one-week free trial. Below is a link to their free trial that is being offered at the time this was written. Maybe their free trail will still be available when you check it.

I'll bet you're thinking about waiting for the free trial before you do this. Remember this the next time you're tempted to get your customers addicted to coupons.

https://www.wordtracker.com/trial/

Wordtracker will give you more information about your keywords, but to get the most out of it you need to spend a little time learning their terms and how to use all of the options they make available to you.

Play with all of the above tools and see what you can find out about which keywords and keyword phrases you should be optimizing your website for. There is no need to have a website that is optimized for keyword phrases that no one is searching for.

One last point about keywords: Don't try to optimize your website for a single keyword. There are two reasons for this. First, no one searches for a single word anymore. They search for phrases. The second reason is that the keyword is included within the keyword phrase and you will be optimizing for it anyway when you optimize for the keyword phrase.

Now let's look at an example of what can happen when you have a properly designed website.

How $1.64 a day in Internet marketing brings in an extra $100,000 a year for one restaurant owner (year after year)

Don't let another day go by without implementing this strategy into your restaurant marketing plan. Here's how he did it.

Paul Stephenson, owner of "Kingfisher Seafood and Steakhouse" tracks how his new customers find out about his restaurant.

He consistently finds that over $100,000 worth of new business comes in every year from people who found his restaurant on the Internet.

Paul pays someone less than $500 a year to maintain his website. This comes out to $1.64 a day for generating $100,000 in new business every year.

Maybe this will convince you that you need a website if you don't already have one, and the next section will show you how to do it.

How to have your own restaurant website in 15 minutes and for less than $5 a month

Putting up a website for your restaurant could be your biggest money-making decision of the year. Many restaurant owners report over $10,000 a month in extra sales directly due to their websites.

Setting up your own website is as easy as 1, 2, 3.

Here's step-by-step how to do it:

Step 1. Use the tool www.GoDaddy.com to find the domain name you want. Your first choice will probably be "www.YourRestaurantName.com."

If your first choice for a name is not available, keep searching until you find a name you like. Make sure it's a name that is easy to spell and doesn't use any dashes. **Be sure to select a ".com" name** and **NOT** a ".org" or ".net" or ".info" or ".biz" or any of the other domain name suffixes.

Your goal is to have a domain name that is short, easy to remember and by all means easy to spell.

Step 2. Register the domain name you select with GoDaddy. I've tried several other companies and I believe you will get the best service with **www.GoDaddy.com**. Register the name for at least two years. It saves you a little bit of money and, best of all, Google ranks sites higher that are registered for more than one year. I guess they figure that these are not spam sites that are going to be here today and gone tomorrow. Use GoDaddy to register your Domain name, but don't sign up for any of their other services. Use HostGator to host your website as described below.

Step 3. Host your website with www.HostGator.com. You can host your site for $4.95 a month with their *Hatchling* plan. If you plan on having more than one website (maybe for another business or another Internet project) you can go with their *Baby* plan for only $7.95 and host an unlimited number of websites.

With either plan you can use their free **Site Builder** program to completely build your website in a matter of minutes. You can play with their **Site Builder Demo** at the link below before you even sign up for their service. Go give it a try.

sitebuilder.websitewelcome.com/Wizard

That's all there is to it. Your website will be up and running in a matter of minutes. Don't worry about getting everything just right. You can go back and make changes at any time.

Don't let the sun set on your restaurant again without having your own website. A website tells the world that you are on top of things and know how to manage a restaurant. Your website will soon be bringing you a lot of new customers.

Google usually makes a new website wait six to nine months or longer before they will rank them very high, but you need to get the clock ticking. This is normally referred to as being in the *Google Sandbox*. The other search engines don't do this, so you will start getting some business sooner than the six to nine months.

If you want a more elaborate website design, go to www.eLance.com and post your project. You will get several bids (in the $50 to $100 range) in a matter of minutes. (See

Chapter 12 about how to get a cookbook created this way to sell in your restaurant)

One last point about setting up your website. After you have your website up and running, get two or three of your friends who have websites to put a link to your site on their site. This is important because Google and the other search engines won't index your site until someone links to it. If you have to, give someone a free dinner for two to get them to link to your website. That's a good investment.

If you are a member of your local Chamber of Commerce, let them know you have a website and get them to provide a link to your website. This is a very valuable authority-type link in the eyes of search engines.

Get your restaurant listed free in Google Maps and drive a steady stream of customers to your restaurant

Very few restaurants have taken the time to get listed in Google Maps and people are using Google Maps in ever increasing numbers when they are looking for restaurants.

There are a LOT of people searching for places to dine and there are very few restaurants in Google Maps for them to find. It's a gold mine for the restaurants that get listed.

To make it even more enticing to get your restaurant listed, it's easy and absolutely free. What else can you ask for? Getting listed in Google Maps also creates a LOT of credibility for your restaurant.

It's easy to get your site listed. Here's how to do it:

First, go to **maps.google.com/** and click on "**Put your business on Google Maps**." Log in (or create an account if you don't have one). Then provide the general information about your restaurant and a 200-character description.

Next, decide on a category (Google will help you with this if necessary).

Finally, Google will mail a postcard to you to verify your address. Follow the instructions and in a little over a month your listing will be active. It only takes a few minutes to start the clock ticking.

In addition to driving customers to your restaurant, you can make it even easier for them to find you. You can add a link (or button) on your web site that prospective customers can click on and it will give them detailed driving directions right to your parking lot.

Here's the easy way to place a link on your site to your Google Map

1. After your business is listed and confirmed, go to **Maps.Google.com** again and type your business name into the search window. Your business will come up. Click on the "View larger map" link then click on your listing and then click on the title inside the balloon and your Google Maps page will show up.

2. Copy this URL and paste it on your website where you want the map to show up.

Bottom line: Be one of the first instead of one of the last restaurants to get listed in Google Maps.

How to turn your website into a customer generating machine

The Internet is rapidly becoming a major source of new customers for many restaurants. For almost no money, here's the quick and easy (non-technical) way to turn your website into a machine that generates customers for your restaurant.

More and more customers are checking out restaurants online before they go out to eat. If they don't find your website, your restaurant will not even be considered by these Internet savvy customers. They'll just go to one of your competitors.

It would be nice if your restaurant would come up #1 when someone anywhere in the world searched for the word,

"Restaurant." Stop dreaming. Even McDonald's doesn't have a big enough budget to make that happen.

The good news is that there is a way you can get to the top of the search engines without having to compete with the whole world.

All you have to do to stack the deck in your favor is get your website listed in what is called, "Local Search" by the different search engines.

The good news is that if you have a listing in the regular Yellow Pages (the big yellow paper book), there's a good chance you will already be showing up in the different Internet Local Search databases without any effort on your part, so be sure to check to see if your site is already listed.

Here's how to check to see if you're already listed. Check, you might be lucky.

Google is the most important search engine, so let's start there.

To check your **Google Local** listing, go to. . .

www.Google.com/lochp

Type in the name of your restaurant and see if your restaurant shows up. If there are several restaurants in the US with the same name as your restaurant, you may have to scroll down the list to find your restaurant.

By the way, you can also check

Yahoo Local at **local.yahoo.com/**

And check **MSN Local** at **local.msn.com/**

If your restaurant is not already listed, here's how to get your site listed in the Locals

Your chances of being listed by the Internet Local Search databases are greatly improved by being listed in the most important Internet Yellow Pages.

There are a dozen Internet Yellow Pages. You don't need to be listed with all of them. Start by submitting to the free business profile at **www.SuperPages.com** and if you want to get even more publicity, you could buy the cheapest listing (a basic business card at $12 a month) with **www.YellowPages.com**. You can be listed without doing this and paying the $12 a month, but there are other benefits to being listed here.

This will get you picked up and ranked in the major Local Search databases of the Internet Yellow Pages. Be sure to list your information exactly the same way in every listing on your website and the Local Search databases will have fewer problems with your listing.

Back to Google

If your restaurant is new or if you are having trouble getting listed for some reason, here's how to get in the Google Local Search listings in a hurry. Google gets data from their own pages (of course) and from the different Internet Yellow Pages. That's why it helps to be listed with one or more of the Internet Yellow Pages.

Here's the next step that's important:

It's important to have your information on EVERY page of your website. The best way to do this is to include the information in a footer. Keep it simple like this and in this format:

Bill's Seafood and Steakhouse
100 Sanders Ferry Rd.
Hendersonville, TN 37075
1-800-123-4567

One last point: you can edit or add your listing to Google's Local Search by going to **Google Local Business Center** (**https://www.google.com/local/add/login**). Follow the instructions. Go through the few steps involved then Google will send you a letter containing a PIN and instructions showing you how to make the changes to your listings.

Here are a few misc. notes about additional basic steps to getting your restaurant website ranked even higher in the local search directories and in the search engines in general.

> **Note:** Some of these techniques have already been discussed in other sections, but in order for this section to stand alone, I am repeating some of the information and techniques here.

These techniques are important and worth reading two times anyway.

1. Most people don't search for a single word. They search for phrases and sometimes long phrases. For example, instead of searching for "restaurant" they would more than likely search for exactly what they're looking for like, "Dallas seafood restaurant" or maybe, "Seafood restaurants in Dallas."

(Note: Singular and plural versions of words are treated as different words by most search engines, so be sure to use both "restaurant" and "restaurants" on your website and in your Title.)

2. Make sure the three to five keyword phrases that people might search for are used on the Home page of your website. For example: "Atlanta BBQ restaurant," "BBQ ribs," "BBQ catering" and use all of the different ways of spelling any keywords, such as BBQ, bar-b-que, barbecue and barbeque. Upper and lower case doesn't matter.

3. Also, make sure these keyword phrases are included in what is called your Title tag. Your Title tag is **not** the same as the headline for your web page. Get your webmaster to do this for you if this sounds like Greek to you.

4. Get other websites to link to your website using your important keyword phrases in the anchor text. If you want to know more about anchor text and how to use it, go to Wikipedia (the online encyclopedia) at

en.wikipedia.org/wiki/Anchor_text

Getting other BBQ restaurants in other cities (that are not competing with your BBQ restaurant) to link to your website is a good way to get on-topic incoming links.

Swap links with them if you have to, but it's **much** better to get a link without having to use reciprocal links. Swapping free dinners for links is much better. Search engines don't count reciprocal links nearly as much as one-way links.

Bottom line: Make sure your business is listed in Google's Local Search and Google Maps. Those are two of the most important things you can do to get business from the Internet.

How to market your restaurant with Free YouTube Videos

If you haven't heard of or looked at any **YouTube** videos, stop right now and go to **www.YouTube.com** and see what you're missing. Google recently paid $1.6 billion dollars to buy this company. That's billion with a "B." You can bet YouTube is going to be big. In fact, it is already big. Over 100,000 new videos a day are being added and that number will be way out of date by the time you read this.

The best part about YouTube is that it is all free and it is so easy to put your two to three minute videos on YouTube. I'm sure several people on your staff already know how to do this. You can shoot videos with almost any regular digital camera made now. Or for about $50 to $100 you can get on eBay and buy what is called a "flip camcorder" or "pocket video camera." This type of camcorder is made to order to shoot YouTube videos. It has a USB port built in. It plugs directly into your computer and the software is included.

You can also go to almost any store that carries electronics or office supply and get this type of camcorder for about $100 to $200. YouTube accepts widescreen (16:9 ratio) videos now. The older 4:3 size videos are starting to look a little outdated, so go with a camcorder that shoots the widescreen format. YouTube also accepts high definition (HD) videos, but these are slower to load. I would go with the standard defination (SD) and the widescreen format.

Search YouTube for "Restaurant [your town]" and see what comes up. Maybe one of your competitors will be showing off their restaurant, but not many of them if any, I bet.

It's easy to add titles and narration to your YouTube videos. Complete instructions are included on the YouTube site, and as I said before, I'm sure members of your staff already know how to do all of this.

You don't have to stop with one video. You can put up videos every week or even every day. A lot of people are spending several hours a day watching YouTube videos instead of watching TV. You owe it to yourself to go check out some of these videos.

You could put up a video showing how to make hush puppies or how to cook salmon or just show the inside and outside of your restaurant. If you have live entertainment, shoot a short two or three minute video of the entertainment and show people having a good time at your restaurant. You can delete a video anytime you decide you don't like it.

As an added bonus, Google is now listing YouTube Videos on the first page in the top 10 websites that come up for a lot of searches. This is one easy way to get your restaurant to show up on the first page of Google.

Some YouTube videos get hundreds of thousands of views. YouTube shows you how many people have viewed any particular video. It could be kind of fun to check in every now and then and see how many people have viewed each of your videos and see the comments they have added.

Be sure to check the box that says, "Allow comments after I approve them." Otherwise you will get a lot of spam comments.

You can also create videos for YouTube without a video camera. Use Microsoft's free PhotoStory3 program to take still photos and make them into a video complete with background music, titles, zooming, etc. To see examples of what can be done with this free software and to download the free software go to:

www.microsoft.com/windowsxp/using/digitalphotogra phy/photostory/default.mspx

And remember, YouTube video marketing is totally FREE.

How to use Internet Directories to market your restaurant

As I've pointed out before, when people search for a new place to eat, more and more of them are searching the Internet.

Will they find your restaurant? The chances of them finding your restaurant will be much better if your restaurant's website is listed in the three important Internet Directories.

You may not be an Internet expert and you may not get (or expect) much of your business to come from the Internet, but a small investment of time and money could change all that.

Getting the right Internet Directories to link to your restaurant's website can make your website rank higher on Google and the other search engines. This will make it more much likely that people searching the Internet will find your website and "discover" your restaurant. But. . .

Not all Internet Directories are created equal.

Most of the free directories that anyone can get listed in may not be worth the time and trouble it takes to get them to list your website.

Look at it from Google's standpoint

If it's free to get listed in a directory and every website is accepted, how does that indicate to Google that a website should be ranked higher just because they are listed in that directory? – It doesn't. That's why Google stopped valuing links from many of these Internet Directories.

There are still a lot of directories that do add value to your website and also drive customers to your website and to your restaurant. These are usually niche directories or regional directories for the restaurant industry or for your geographical area. Or they are the directories that charge a fee and have rules and guidelines about which sites they list.

Here are the facts. Tests have shown that the search engines look at it this way. Search engines figure that if you are at all serious about your restaurant, you will at least be listed in the following three directories:

- **dir.yahoo.com/**
- **www.DMOZ.org**
- **www.Business.com**

If your restaurant website is not listed in these three directories, go to the above websites and get the process started immediately. The steps to get your restaurant's website listed in these three directories are easy and straight forward.

Getting listed in DMOZ is free. (It can take forever sometimes to get listed, but you might as well go ahead and start the process and get the clock ticking.)

Yahoo and Business.com charge a fee to list your website and they don't accept everyone – maybe that's why Google values the websites that do get listed in their directories.

Business.com has the added repetition of providing a lot of real customers for the businesses they list.

Bottom line: Submit your restaurant website to DMOZ immediately and as soon as your budget will allow it, pay to get listed in the Yahoo Directory (for $297) and in Business.com (for $150) in that order.

Getting listed in these two paid directories would probably cost you less than you're going to waste on your next newspaper ad (and getting listed in these two directories will bring you a lot more business than you will get from most ads). So think seriously about it before you dismiss the idea and say you can't afford to do it right now.

How to get listed at the top of Google's search results absolutely FREE

Maybe this technique won't fill every table in your restaurant every night, but it just might. You can quickly get your restaurant listed at the very top of the Google search results on the Internet. You can do this without knowing anything about computers or anything about the Internet.

Whether you love it, hate it or just don't know much about it, the Internet is fast becoming a major player when it comes to bringing customers into restaurants. And you can bet that the Internet influence is going to be getting stronger every day.

More and more visitors and locals alike are now searching the Internet to find information about restaurants in the area before they go out to eat.

When someone does a search like, "Dallas restaurants" or "Restaurants in Chicago, IL" (and you have a restaurant in the city being searched for), it would be great if your restaurant website showed up at the very top of the first page of search results.

Up until now getting listed at the top of the list has been hard to next to impossible for small independent restaurants. You had to have a **lot** of incoming links to your website to make this happen – but not anymore if you use the following technique.

Now there is an easy way to quickly get ranked at the top of the Google search results – even if you don't know anything about computers or the Internet

Here's how:

In the last few years Google has started valuing links from what they call, "Trusted sites" much more than from unknown or untrusted sites. For example, if you got a link from CNN that would be a lot better than a link from a local farmer who sells you fresh vegetables.

Now it looks like Google has decided that sites that allow customers to post reviews of restaurants are "Trusted" sites. So all you have to do is get some reviews about your restaurant posted on some of the popular review sites.

Let me show you what reviews on these review sites can do for you. Google has started showing what they call their "**10-listing One Box**" at the very top of their search results when people search for restaurants.

When I searched Google for "Asheville restaurants," the results below appeared at the very top of the search results page. The restaurants are generally shown from top to bottom based on the number of reviews posted, but not exactly. This is because Google values reviews from some sites more than from other sites.

Local business results for **Restaurants** near **Asheville, N Carolina**

A. Tupelo Honey Cafe - www.tupelohoneycafe.com - (828) 255-4863 - 97 reviews
B. Mela Indian **Restaurant** - www.melaasheville.com - (828) 225-8880 - 20 reviews
C. Olive Garden Italian **Restaurant** - www.olivegarden.com - (828) 255-9887 - 6 reviews
D. Red Lobster **Restaurants** - www.redlobster.com - (828) 350-7773 - 5 reviews
E. Flying Frog Wine Bar & Cafe - www.flyingfrogcafe.com - (828) 254-9411 - 17 reviews
F. Corner Kitchen - www.thecornerkitchen.com - (828) 274-2439 - 44 reviews
G. Biltmore Estate - www.biltmore.com - (800) 922-0091 - 345 reviews
H. Thai Basil **Restaurant** - www.thaibasilnc.com - (828) 258-0036 - 4 reviews
I. Cornerstone **Restaurant** - www.cornerstonerest.com - (828) 236-0201 - 13 reviews
J. IHOP **Restaurant** - www.ihop.com - (828) 255-8601 - 3 reviews

More results near **Asheville, N Carolina »**

Notice that it took as few as 3 reviews to get a restaurant listed in this **10-listing One Box** in Asheville. (Hint: you probably have more employees than that.)

Now take a look at the results for a larger city. Below is the box that showed up when I searched for "Orlando restaurants." Even in a large city like Orlando, Florida, you can be listed in the "**10-listing One Box**" with only 14 reviews. See the screenshot below:

Local business results for **Restaurants** near **Orlando, FL**

A. Hue **Restaurant** - www.huerestaurant.com - (407) 849-1800 - 51 reviews
B. Little Saigon **Restaurant** Inc - www.littlesaigonrestaurant.com - (407) 423-8539 - 26 reviews
C. Garden Cafe' Vegetarian **Restaurant** - www.gardencafevege.com - (407) 999-9799 - 27 reviews
D. Amura Japanese **Restaurant** - www.amura.com - (407) 316-8500 - 67 reviews
E. Harp And Celt **Restaurant** And Irish Pub - www.harpandcelt.com - (407) 481-2928 - 14 reviews
F. Olive Garden Italian **Restaurant** - www.olivegarden.com - (407) 896-0498 - 25 reviews
G. Doc's **Restaurant** - www.docsrestaurant.com - (407) 839-3627 - 15 reviews
H. Viet Garden **Restaurant** - www.vietgardenorlando.com - (407) 896-4154 - 14 reviews
I. Ceviche Tapas Bar & **Restaurant** - www.ceviche.com - (321) 281-8140 - 21 reviews
J. Royal Thai **Restaurant** - www.royalthai-orlando.com - (407) 275-0776 - 27 reviews

More results near **Orlando, FL »**

I checked some smaller cities and when searching Google for "Columbia SC restaurants," I found that you can be in the Top-10 Box with only ONE review.

Note that for cities that have the same city name in different states, it may be necessary to include the state in your search like in the above example for Columbia, SC.

Even if your town is not yet listed, it's worth your while to start getting reviews posted. Google is adding more cities and towns all the time and they are probably valuing these trusted review sites as one of the many factors they look at when deciding where in the list to rank restaurants even when they don't show a 10-listing One Box.

I checked Nashville, Tennessee, which has millions of visitors a year going there for the Grand Ole Opry and the country music tours, etc. All of these people are going to be eating out. A restaurant can get in the Top-10 Box in Nashville with only 32 reviews.

You probably have this many employees and friends who would post a review for you – particularly if you have their spouses post a review also.

Where do visitors need to go to place their reviews? Below is an alphabetical list of 21 sites that Google is currently getting data from. The following 21 sources accept public reviews as of now, but check them out because they do change their rules from time to time.

10best.com
Aol.com
ChefMoz.org
Citysearch.com
Dine.com
DiningGuide.com
Dinnerbroker.com
Frommers.com
Greenopia.com
Insiderpages.com
Menupages.com

Mytravelguide.com
Priceline.com
RestaurantRow.com
Travelocity.com
Travelpost.com
TripAdvisor.com
Virtualtourist.com
Yahoo.com
Yelp.com
Zagat.com

You (or one of your employees) should post a review of your restaurant (using slightly different words) to **each** of the sites below. This will let you know for sure that they are currently accepting public reviews for restaurants in your area.

www.TripAdvisor.com is a very powerful and trusted site in Google's eyes. The number of reviews I found coming from this source was substantial. So this is a great place to send visitors.

Yelp, Insiderpages and Citysearch are now back on Google's trusted list and are good places to have reviews posted.

Don't have all of your reviews coming from just one review site and don't give people a script to use. You don't want all of your reviews sounding exactly alike.

Here's how to take action immediately:

At your next employee meeting you (or one of your employees) should explain the process of posting reviews (and the benefit to your restaurant). Then if possible, have someone actually go through the process and demonstrate how to post a review of your restaurant on one of the review sites.

After you show them how, ask each employee to post at least one review using their home computer when they go home. Also, ask them to ask their spouse or roommate to post a review. Then follow up the next day (and the following day) to see how many of them did post a review. Let them know how important it is.

If you have a mailing list (email or regular mail), send out a request asking all of your customers to post reviews for you. Consider handing out cards to your guests showing them exactly how, where and why to post a review of your restaurant.

One last point: Now people can use their cell phones to rate your restaurant. If a guy thinks you are slow bringing out his food, he can pull out his cell phone, click on the city and then on the list of restaurants, click on your restaurant and give you a bad rating. It's that simple. As more people become familiar with how to do this, you could be getting a lot of reviews and they may not all be good. How should you deal with this problem? The best way to keep a bad review from hurting your restaurant is to have a ton of great positive reviews to offset the one or two bad reviews. Just one more reason why you should take steps to start getting positive reviews stacked up in your corner now.

Bottom line: Get some reviews posted about your restaurant and you will soon have large crowds coming to your restaurant. This will cost you absolutely nothing and it will pay bigger and bigger dividends for years to come. Having reviews posted about your restaurant on the Internet is getting more valuable every day. Take action now and leave your competition in the dust.

Be one of the first restaurants (and not one of the last) restaurant managers to take advantage of the Internet to drive a starving crowd to your restaurant.

What could you do this week to bring more customers into your restaurant than to start the process of getting reviews posted about your restaurant?

## Chapter 10

Press Releases

In this chapter I'm going to show you how to use press releases to fill every seat and never spend another dime on advertising.

Use one of these 13 press release headlines and stories I'll give you later in this chapter and you will have all the customers you could ever want. The news media is more than willing to make you as wealthy as you want to be if you will just give them what they want – a good story.

An ad is you telling how wonderful your restaurant is – an article in the newspaper or other media is the editor, writer or host telling the world what a wonderful restaurant you have.

A good publicity campaign will do two things: it will bring you immediate sales and it will continue to bring you sales for a long time – maybe even years.

The goal of all of your press releases should be to get across the message that you offer a better dining experience than your competitors. Do it right and this message will come across without you ever having to say it.

People want more than just good food at a good price. If that's all they wanted, they would go visit their mother and get some good home cooking and it would be free. When people go out to eat, they are looking for a great dining experience. Good food, good service, and a good price are all part of that.

Here's how the press release game is played. You give the editor a story that will interest his or her readers and he or she will give you publicity. That's all there is to it.

Most of the stories that newspapers and the media publish are not news stories. Who would want to read a story with a headline that says, "River floods – no damage," but how about, "River floods, hundreds homeless, three people still missing." Most people's lives are boring. They look to the media to find excitement.

As Al Neuharth, the guy who started *USA Today*, said, "When you read a headline if it doesn't make you say, "Holy Sh**! Did you see this?" It's NOT a good headline.

The story in your press release (and especially, the headline) has to evoke Al Neuharth's, "Holy Sh**" reaction or else your story will not get published. It's that simple.

Later we will talk about exactly how to write a press release and how to get it to the editors, and even include some sample press releases you can use, but let's start at the beginning and look at some headlines.

Most press releases fall into one of four categories. Below is a description of each of the four categories along with some sample headlines you can use for each. I have also included a sentence or two with each headline telling you more about how to use the headline. The first type of headline is when you. . .

Reveal a Secret:

A secret is anything you know that the general public doesn't know (which is just about everything about the restaurant industry). Consider the following headlines that fall into this category:

Why homeless shelters celebrate as wedding season approaches

A lot of restaurants donate the leftover food from tasting sessions and wedding receptions to the homeless shelters.

How to make sure you always get the best table in any restaurant

Just say, "We're celebrating." Restaurant owners and managers always like to help people celebrate. Maybe you're just celebrating a good day or a fun evening with friends, but you can always find something to celebrate. I've amazed friends many times when I have used this technique. It almost always works and we get the best table in the house.

Why local farmers are celebrating as restaurant changes menus

The new menu will include more locally grown fresh fruits and vegetables.

News stories:

Cash in on popular news stories by piggy backing your story onto a hot news story.

When a hot story comes out that the public is interested in, the media will beat it to death telling the same thing over and over because they don't have anything new to tell. Give the media a new twist about how the story ties in with your restaurant and your story will get published.

When you're reading the newspaper or watching the news on TV **always** be asking yourself, "How can I tie that story into what's going on in my restaurant?" Here are some examples of how to do this:

Do jury members really keep quiet about the Smith case while they're eating in restaurants?

Everyone wonders about this and the newspapers and TV stations have run out of things to say about this popular local trial. Explain how you instruct your servers to not ask questions and make sure no other guests are allowed to violate the judge's instructions while jurors are eating in your restaurant.

Local farmers celebrate as hotel changes menu

The new menu will feature more locally grown produce. (Note: This headline is a modified version of one we used in the "secret" category.)

Retiring high school coach honored with restaurant dining room named after him

Renaming one of your dining rooms after a popular, well liked local public figure will always get you publicity.

Fun stories:

Local restaurant conducts a coffee bean poll to select the next mayor with surprising results

Everyone who orders a cup of coffee at Charlie's Cafe between now and election time gets one coffee bean to drop into one of the three fruit jars sitting by the cash register. (They now call them point-of-sale terminals, but they're still cash registers to me.) There's a jar for each of the three mayor candidates.

A running tally is kept and a new total is posted every Wednesday at 7:00 A.M.. The beans in each jar are counted every Tuesday night by the bean counters at the local CPA firm of Dewey, Cheatem and Howe. (Give your CPA a little free publicity and he will feel indebted to you.)

You can use this technique for both local and national political races. The news media will jump all over this story. They are always looking for a new twist on a political story. You may get more than one story out of this as the newspapers and TV stations come back to see what the new count is each week.

Glasses and cell phones top list of forgot items at restaurants – Wives and mother-in-laws are also left behind

(That's what happened last week when John Jones drove off and forgot and left his wife at Joe's Steakhouse. John said he thought she had already caught a ride with some friends.)

The news media has been known to do more than just report the news. Sometimes they help a little to create the news. If the incident above has not actually happened at your restaurant yet (and I 'm betting that it has), rather than waiting until it does happen again, you could have someone help shorten your wait time.

Local restaurant helps a young man turn proposal into an offer no girl could refuse

I'm sure you've had guys pop the question after a wonderful dinner at your restaurant. If not – find someone who is about to get engaged and promise to make it a special event for him at your restaurant. Help make the story happen if you have to.

Charity and Community Stories:

Politicians have found that they can get the media to write stories about them if they stage an event (like a rally, etc.). You can do the same thing. Consider the following headlines or variation of them.

Local restaurant to host fund raiser for Black Mountain volunteer fire department

On Saturday May the 10th from 10 A.M. until 4 P.M., The Cellar Door restaurant will be hosting a fund raiser to benefit the Black Mountain volunteer fire department. There will be live music supplied by the "Old Timers Band," six-foot long deli sandwiches with pieces being sold and all proceeds going to the fire department. There will also be a fire truck parked in the parking lot and the children can climb into the cab and see the all the controls and even have their pictures taken. There will be contests and prizes awarded all day – and on and on.

Get a second story out of this after the event is over with a headline like this:

The Cellar Door restaurant raises $3,212 for Black Mountain volunteer fire department

Just describe what went on and how the money was raised and described all of the activities and events that went on and maybe tell what the fire department plans to do with the money.

The key to a good press release is to think about what you can do to shock the local and even the national media into taking notice.

How about a charity event where the mayor and all of the city council members are given poker chips to play poker in your back room and the winner gets to cash his chips in and the proceeds go to a local charity? You could have a headline like. . .

Mayor and city council members caught playing poker in back room of local restaurant

or

Gambling hall opens in downtown Harrisburg

These headlines should get some attention. Then go on to explain how your restaurant is sponsoring the event to raise money for whatever.

Conclusions:

The news media are more than willing to make you as wealthy as you want to be if you will just give them what they want – a good story.

I have given you 13 headlines and story ideas you can use. Add your facts and information to these stories and you will have a press release ready for every week for the next three months. By then you'll be cranking out your own headlines and stories.

You should mix up your press releases. Send out a news story one week and a fun story the next, etc. Once you get into the rhythm of writing and sending out press releases, it will become a habit – and a very profitable habit at that.

One last point: Keep in mind that it is **not** the purpose of your press release to tell your whole story. What you want your press release to do is to get an editor's attention and get him or her interested enough in your story to come out and interview you and make some pictures. If pictures are taken, you are almost sure to get a half-page to a full-page story out of it.

If the editor just uses the information included in your press release, you can be sure your story will be very small. Of course, that beats nothing, but what you really want is a large feature story out of your press release.

In the next section I will show you some sample press releases you can use by adding your information and by making minor changes to fit your situation. Don't worry that every other restaurant owner who has this book will be using these same press releases because most people are like the three birds sitting on a fence in the story below:

If three birds were sitting on a fence and one decided to fly away, how many would be left?

Probably all three – just because one bird decided to fly away doesn't mean that he actually did it. And just because we as humans decide to do something, doesn't mean that it will actually be done. Sending out a press release will probably still be on most restaurant owners' "To Do" list when the list is lost or replaced by a new list.

After you look at the sample press releases, I will show you step-by-step how to write your press releases starting with the format (which is absolutely essential that you have right) and then how to write the first paragraph. And the second. On down to the last line to the final three "# # #" at the end. With this format, it will almost be like filling in the blanks every week and you will have another press release.

And I will cover the important parts about where and how to send out your press releases, too.

Sample press releases that bring in business

But now let's take a look at some sample press releases. While you're reading these press releases be thinking about how you can modify them to fit your situation and you will be well on your way to having some attention-getting press releases.

FOR FURTHER INFORMATION
CONTACT JILL SMITH
(123) 456-7890

Glasses are most forgotten item at restaurants. . .
spouses and mother-in-laws are left sometimes too!

People are always leaving things at restaurants. The traditional things are glasses, cell phones and coats. But some diners have been known to leave their spouses and one person even left a mother-in-law.

Jill Smith, general manager of the Jill's Seafood restaurant in Lexington, PA said it happened again recently at her restaurant when frequent guest, Wayne Jones accidentally left his wife, Judy at the restaurant.

Wayne and a group of his friends boarded his boat and left his lake front home to head across the lake to Jill's Seafood for dinner one Saturday afternoon. After dinner they were all talking and having a good time when someone noticed it looked like it was about to rain.

They all hurried to get on the boat and get back across the lake before the rain started and the water got choppy. As soon as everyone was on board, Wayne took off back across the lake.

When he arrived at his boat dock, he noticed that his wife, Judy wasn't on board. He called the Jill's Seafood restaurant and was told that yes, she was sitting there waiting to see when he would miss her. "I don't know if Wayne is out of the doghouse yet or not" Jill said, "But I bet he won't make that mistake again – at least, not any time soon."

When first questioned, Jill said, "I can't remember anytime someone has left a mother-in-law at my restaurant." But then Jill said, "On second thought, Wayne and Judy's daughter is married, so that makes Judy someone's mother-in-law. So I guess I can say a mother-in-law has been left at Jill's Seafood restaurant after all."

For more information, call Jill Smith at (123) 456-7890 for a fun and informative interview.

#

Why Homeless Shelters Will Have Reason to Celebrate as the Holiday Season Gets Closer

Homeless shelters in Columbus, OH will have a reason to be celebrating as the Holiday Season rolls around this year because the Blue Anchor restaurant plans on donating the food left over from the many Christmas and New Year's parties and banquets this year. This means the local residents who are down on their luck will be receiving top quality food – and indirectly be taking part in the local celebrations.

"We always prepare about 20% extra food for these festive occasions in case extra guests show up and to make sure there is always enough food to go around," explains Todd Johnson, general manager of the Blue Anchor restaurant on the lake in Columbus.

"Instead of throwing out the mountains of leftovers this year, we have arranged with the homeless shelter in Columbus to have them come and take it away because it would break my heart to see good food going to waste," Todd said.

Among the festive food that the local homeless will be enjoying this year are top-quality roasts, seasonal and exotic vegetables as well as mousses, cakes and cookies.

As a result of this effort, a homeless person in Columbus can expect to enjoy festive fare at least once a week during the early part of the season and as often as every night in December.

To discover how charities benefit from banquets and for an informative and entertaining interview, call Todd Johnson at (123) 456-7890.

# # #

FOR FURTHER INFORMATION
CONTACT JAMES OWENS
(123) 456-7890

Restaurant Plans Festive Event to Raise Money for the Macon Volunteer Fire Department

The Rusty Pelican restaurant on the lake in Macon, GA will be hosting activities Saturday, Oct. 13th from 10:00 A.M. To 4:00 P.M. to raise money to help support the Macon Volunteer Fire Department. The money will be used to make repairs to the fire station and to provide much needed equipment.

James Owens, general manager of the Rusty Pelican said, "Live music will be provided by the *New Horizons* band and they are donating their services."

James also added, "The events planned include a staff egg-and-spoon race and waiters and waitresses racing to deliver drinks though an obstacle course of old tires and steps, and there will be lots of games, such as sack races, for both the grownups and for the kids."

The Rusty Pelican will be providing popcorn shrimp, hush puppies, three-foot long sandwiches (cut in smaller pieces, of course) and a lot of other food. All of the profits will be donated to the fire department. Lots of new and used items will be auctioned off with all of the proceeds going to the fire department. People are encouraged to bring items early and donate them so then can be auctioned off at 2:00 P.M.

The head chef of the Rusty Pelican is being auctioned off to come to your home. He'll bring the food and prepare a gourmet meal for you and up to eight of your guests. Other businesses and professionals are encouraged to donate their services or products to be auctioned off.

The fire truck will be parked in the parking lot and children will be allowed to climb into the cab, see the controls and even have their pictures taken.

For more information and an entertaining interview, call James Owens at (123) 456-7890.

# # #

FOR FURTHER INFORMATION
CONTACT BILL TAYLOR
(123) 456-7890

"Can You Paint the Dining Room Green, Please?" Voted Year's Weirdest Restaurant Request

Wedding planners will tell you that brides are known for making strange requests when it comes to planning their weddings. But when it comes to planning the reception dinner and the rehearsal dinner, restaurant managers are the ones who get to hear the really weird requests.

Bill Taylor, general manager of the Bill's Steakhouse restaurant in Dallas, TX said his management staff has voted the weirdest request so far this year to be the one from the bride who asked if they could paint the dining room green to match the color of her bridesmaids' dresses.

Bill said that it really wasn't as far-fetched of a request as it might sound, because they would probably have accommodated her request if they had not just recently repainted the inside of the restaurant – and green was one of the colors they were considering. But since the restaurant was on the lake and they wanted to keep the water theme, they had gone with blue. Then Bill added, "But who in their right mind thinks the lake around here is ever blue."

Other interesting requests have been, "Can you make an ice cream cake and serve it outside on the deck for my August wedding reception?" And another one was, "Can the servers dress to match the theme of my wedding?"

Bill added, "We have been happy to accommodate all of these requests and looking back, I wish I had painted the restaurant green for the bride who requested it. Maybe the next time I will."

For more information, call Bill Taylor at (123) 456-7890 for a fun and informative interview.

# # #

FOR IMMEDIATE RELEASE

FOR FURTHER INFORMATION
CONTACT SARAH WILLIAMS
(123) 456-7890

Restaurant Collects $2,317 to Support Local Animal Shelter

The Blue Ridge Bistro was the site of a lot of activity last Saturday as they hosted a fun event to raise money to support the local animal shelter. Altogether they raised $2,317, which will be used to update the facilities and help take care of and treat the more than 200 abandoned and abused animals at the overcrowded Lexington Animal Shelter.

Sarah Williams, general manager of the Blue Ridge Bistro said the event was a huge success and they plan to make it an annual event. Sarah added, "Having the dogs and cats there (along with a lot of puppies and kittens) was a big hit with the children. The best part," she said, "was that many of the adorable animals found new homes Saturday as the children fell in love with them."

James Akins, director of the Lexington Animal Shelter, said that he was happy to see all of the community support. James added, "The much-needed $2,317 donation was greatly appreciated because the Animal Shelter has not been expanded in over ten years and the number of animals housed is now more than double what the facility was originally designed for."

"The day was a blast," said Sarah. "We had over 300 people stop by during the day to make donations and take part in the activities, but we couldn't have made it happen without the help of the many volunteers from the community and from the Animal Shelter." She added, "I'm already looking forward to next year's event."

For more information, call Sarah Williams at (123) 456-7890 for a fun and informative interview.

# # #

FOR FURTHER INFORMATION
CONTACT JENNY WILSON
(123) 456-7890

Wedding Guests keep cool with ice cream wedding cakes

As the summer heats up and weddings head outside and into the sun and heat, brides are breaking with tradition and the year's big hit is turning out to be. . . ice cream wedding cakes. And as you might guess, the guests love it.

Jenny Wilson, manager of Jenny's Restaurant, said, "I was surprised the first time a bride asked if we could provide an ice cream wedding cake, but I discussed it with my chef and he said he could do it and we have been providing ice cream wedding cakes ever since."

"The cakes come in three and five tier versions and have three layers of ice cream. The most requested flavors are the traditional vanilla, strawberry and chocolate flavors with frozen icing, but some brides have been even more non-traditional and asked for some exotic ice cream flavors. We've been able to fulfill every request so far," Jenny said.

"Of course, despite the unconventional ingredients, we still give the cake a somewhat traditional look by having the little bride and groom standing on the top layer."

"Since we started providing the ice cream wedding cake, it has been our most requested cake this year. We bring it out just a little bit later than usual and the couple can still have the fun of cutting the cake and passing out slices to the guests," she said.

For more information, call Jenny Wilson at (123) 456-7890 for a fun and informative interview.

# # #

FOR FURTHER INFORMATION
CONTACT DON WHITE
(123) 456-7890

Whether you're in the doghouse or just want to impress someone special, a very private themed dining room might do the trick

From Yuppies to the retiring baby boomers, people are getting more nostalgic. They seem to want to relive (if only for an evening) a time in their lives that holds fond memories for them.

Don White, owner and manager of Don's Restaurant, said, "I was surprised when someone called and asked if we had a small, romantic private dining room just for two. The man said he and his wife were going to celebrate their 25th wedding anniversary soon and he wanted to make it very special. I thought for a moment and said, "Yes, we do have a room like that. What date would you like to reserve it for?"

Of course, we didn't have a special private dining room, but we had a large closet that wasn't being used. I cleaned it out, had it painted, installed a light dimmer and brought in a beautiful antique table and two chairs that I had in storage. I took the door down and put up a velvet curtain and presto! We had a romantic private dining room for the special occasion. I brought in a little Bose™ radio and CD player to provide just the right music for the special occasion. Now sometimes people bring in their own special CD.

Since that first night the room has grown in popularity and we have added themes and have different murals, pictures, posters and decorations to really make special evenings seem amazingly real. We can provide themes for Casablanca, Elvis, Gone With The Wind, the Caribbean and several more. If we don't have what the customer wants, we try to create it. There's no extra charge for the room, Don said. You just have to reserve it far enough in advance to make sure it's available for your special night. "We even have a get out of the doghouse theme that seems to work wonders," Don said.

For more information, call Don White at (123) 456-7890 for a fun and an informative interview.

# # #

124

The mechanics of how to write a great press release

Now that we have looked at some press releases, let's look step-by-step at the format you should use to write your press releases. **The format is very important. Don't deviate from it.** We will start at the top and go down the page.

The first part should be done in all caps and formatted exactly as shown in the sample press releases. It is **very** important that the phone number will actually reach the person listed. Your cell phone might be a good number to use. A reporter is not going to spend time chasing you down. Don't have someone answer the phone and say that they will have the person listed get back to them. The reporter will not wait. He will just go write another story.

The next part is your headline. Don't use all caps for the headline. It is acceptable to capitalize the first letter of each word if you want to. Make your headline large print and in bold.

After the attention-getting headline you will need a first paragraph that summarizes the story. This first paragraph needs to pull the reader into the story and tell the editor what the story is all about. **If the reporter doesn't know what the story is about after reading the first paragraph, he or she will probably not read any further.**

The second paragraph is very important, also. After you have told the reporter what the story is about, the second paragraph should be a direct quote from you. It tells the editor that he or she has an expert source for the story and it makes the story more lively and dramatic.

Another purpose of this second paragraph is that when the reporter quotes you in his or her story, you will be guaranteed to get the publicity as the source of the quote. Writing this paragraph is easy. Just use your own words. You don't want it to sound like something from a reporter. The quote should describe in your own words what has happened, what you have done or what you are about to do. That's all there is to it.

Take the second paragraph in the sample press releases and change the words to describe your story and you will have a great second paragraph.

Use the rest of the page to tell a little bit more about your story (but keep in mind that it is **not** the purpose of the press release to tell your complete story). By all means, **keep your press release to a single page.**

I have summarized these points and a few more in an easy to follow outline below.

The Nine Elements of a Great Press Release

1. The top part of the press release should use the exact format shown in the sample press releases for the "FOR IMMEDIATE RELEASE" and the contact information. The contact information absolutely must be a phone number that will reach the contact person – ideally the number should be answered by the contact person. A cell phone is great for this.

2. Next have a powerful and compelling one or two line headline centered in large bold print.

3. The first paragraph should completely summarize your story and tell what it is about.

4. The second paragraph should be a direct quote from you telling what happened, what you are going to do or what you have done.

5. The rest of the press release should give a few more intriguing details about the story and include a few more quotes by you.

6. Keep the press release to a single page. This is an absolute must.

7. Double space the press release and include an extra blank line between the paragraphs. If you have to, you can single space the last paragraph or two or use one and a half line spacing instead of double spacing to squeeze a little more information onto the single page.

8. The last paragraph should always start with, "For more information. . ." and give the contact information again. It should be the same information that was given at the top of the press release.

9. The very last line of the press release should be three number signs separated by a space between (like this # # #) and they should be centered. (See the bottom of each of the sample press releases.) This does two things: It tells the reader that it is the end of the press release and it also tells the editor that he or she is dealing with a professional who knows how to write a press release.

Follow the above format, directions and sample press releases and you can turn out compelling press releases that will get you a ton of free publicity.

This free publicity will create an impression of service, dedication and expertise for you and your restaurant and build a brand that is recognized in your community and. . .

Your free stories in the newspapers, magazines, on the radio and on TV will establish that your restaurant is the place in town to go to have a wonderful dining experience. Your competitors can run all of the paid ads they want to and they won't be able to get this same message and impression across about their restaurants. Their ads will just sound like them blowing their own horns.

One last point: You should fax your press releases to the newspaper, magazines, radio and TV stations. Do not send them to a person's attention. The person getting the fax will know who to deliver it to.

It's also a good idea to have a sheet with a list of questions already prepared (of course, questions that you can answer). This is particularly important for radio and TV stations that want to do live interviews with you.

You also want to have what's called a "Bio" ready, which is a sheet telling about you. Most of the time you won't need this, but by all means know the term and you can put one together quickly if you have to.

To really learn to be an expert at writing and using Press Releases, get **Paul Hartunian's "Million Dollar Publicity Kit"** at **www.MillionDollarPublicity.com**. Paul is the world's foremost authority on getting free publicity. I have received thousands and thousands of dollars worth of free publicity by using his simple and straightforward techniques and you can too. In fact, a lot of the information I presented in this article I learned from Paul.

How a press story can bring a flood of customers in within minutes

Below is an example of free publicity that brought a flood of new and existing customers in the door within minutes. Here's how they did it and how you can accomplish the same thing at zero net cost.

I was visiting my mother this morning and we were having coffee and watching the local morning news on TV. (I rarely watch TV news at home, but my mother was watching it when I went in.)

The local news had a segment saying, the local Starbucks™ was giving away free coffee from 9:00 A.M. until 9:30 A.M this morning.

How much coffee could they give away in 30 minutes? Not much. And most people would buy something to go with their coffee anyway, so bottom line, I'm sure the net cost of giving away the free coffee wasn't really a cost, but a profit.

In addition to making a little extra money this morning, they got free publicity showing video footage of their business and telling where they were located. And most important, I'm sure they got a lot of new customers in addition to their regular customers and some of the new customers will become regulars.

I only saw it on the morning news, but someone told me they saw it on the evening news last night, also. You can bet that all of this free publicity was the result of someone faxing a simple press release to the local TV stations.

How you can expand on this idea for your restaurant

How about using April 15th (US income tax deadline) to help you get free publicity?

The news media are always looking for a new twist for something to talk about when it comes to the April 15th income tax deadline. They always show the line at the post office, etc. – basically, they show the same thing every year because they don't have anything new to talk about.

Since a lot of people will be staying up late doing their taxes on the night of April 15th, how about offering free coffee on the morning of April 16th for a short period of time? That would get you on the news.

Think about it—what could you give away that would get your restaurant on the local evening and morning news? Add a different twist to it and maybe you could get on the news every month.

For example, give away free coffee to all Veterans on Veterans Day or to all fathers on Father's Day, and to all mothers on Mother's Day, etc. Make it your goal to find a way to get your restaurant featured on your local news this month and then try to do something every month or so to get on the news.

With these techniques you can do what Starbucks™ did and only give away the free coffee for 30 minutes and still get free publicity.

The key to getting free publicity is to give the news media something to talk about and you will get free publicity.

## Chapter 11

How to Have a Customer-Grabbing Outdoor Sign on a Shoestring Budget

Your outdoor sign can be one of your best or one of your worst marketing investments. Do it right and a small investment will reap huge rewards for years to come.

Do it wrong and you just flushed thousands of dollars down the drain.

Let's look at how to seize the marketing opportunity and avoid the costly pitfalls.

Keep in mind your sign needs to accomplish **two** important things. Don't lose sight of these two goals for your sign and don't let some graphic artist lose your message with fancy, unreadable fonts and graphics.

Here are the two goals your sign needs to accomplish:

Goal #1 for your sign

Your sign should say loud and clear to the world that **this is a restaurant**. In some cases this is easy. The name of your restaurant may already include this message.

For example, Jill's Steakhouse, Joe's Bar and Grill, Main Street Deli and Pizza Bistro all clearly convey the fact that these are restaurants.

But, Famous Joe's, The Salty Dog, Jenny's, and Amigo's could be any type of business – a dress shop, a men's clothing store, a gift shop or even a hardware store.

In some cases the graphics on a sign can convey the message that it's a restaurant. For example, a picture of a chef wearing a chef's hat and holding a pizza or carving a roast clearly conveys the message that it's a restaurant – and even helps convey what kind of restaurant it is.

Another way to convey the message that it's a restaurant is by adding a phrase after the name of the restaurant. (You don't have to actually change the name of your restaurant, just add the phrase below the name.)

For example in the above names, here are some phrases that could be added below the restaurant names:

Famous Joe's
Bar and Grill

The Salty Dog
Restaurant

Jenny's
Steakhouse

Amigo's
Authentic Mexican Food

Goal #2 for your sign

After you have clearly conveyed the message that "this is a restaurant," the next thing you need to do to have an effective **"customer-grabbing sign"** is to convey the type of food, atmosphere and price range you offer.

You can usually do this with the right combination, of restaurant name, graphics and sub-phrase. A sub-phrase is the slightly smaller print you can include just below the name of your restaurant.

Don't try to say too much in your sign or have a really huge sign. In most cases, less is more. As I said before, a graphic design included in your sign showing a chef (wearing a chef's hat) holding a pizza or carving a roast conveys a lot.

Huckfinn's Catfish Restaurant has a sign showing a barefoot boy with a fishing pole over his shoulder. This image along with the name of the restaurant conveys the atmosphere and the kind of food. It also conveys that it's a moderately priced family restaurant. It's not the place you would book to celebrate your wedding anniversary.

"Kingfisher Seafood Restaurant" is a fairly long name and the owner didn't want to make it longer, but by taking out the word, "restaurant" and changing the sign to read, **Kingfisher Seafood and Steakhouse** it conveyed the message that the restaurant was more than just a seafood restaurant.

In almost any group of four or more people, there is almost sure to be someone who isn't really fond of seafood. The name change made the restaurant in the above example appeal to a larger group of people.

Is your restaurant a white tablecloth type of place, a burgers and fries place, a beer and pizza good times place, a Deli, a BBQ restaurant or Steakhouse? Your sign needs to convey this information to be really effective.

Bottom line: Your sign will bring in a lot more customers if you can clearly convey:

> #1. That your business is a restaurant (a lot of signs don't).

> #2. Exactly what it is your restaurant is offering.

Now that you know what it is you want your sign to accomplish, let's talk about **how you can have your killer, crowd-grabbing sign on a very limited budget.**

Here are the steps to designing, buying and installing a powerful sign – along with some pitfalls to avoid.

Let's start at the very beginning. Skip this first step and you could waste thousands of dollars. A **lot** of restaurant owners and managers have learned this the hard way.

The first step is to find out what constraints and restrictions you have to abide by. You don't want to design and install a sign and then find out that it has to come down because you are in violation of some ordinance.

Here are the places to check to see what types of restrictions you have to abide by:

1. Check your lease. There could very likely be some restrictions in your lease about what kind of outside sign you are allowed to put up.

2. Check your city or town ordinances very carefully. You can't assume that if you put up a new sign just like the one you have that it will be OK. Your old sign could have been grandfathered in. Follow city ordinances **very** carefully and jump through **all** the hoops.

I know of one restaurant owner that got his sign designed, approved by the city, had the sign created and installed and then had to take it down, scrap it and start all over because the shade of green in the sign was not what was approved. The city fathers can be very non-forgiving – particularly in Historic Districts.

3. Many shopping areas and malls have rules about signs. Be sure to check.

4. Are you in a Historic District? If so, there are sure to be more restrictions to deal with.

5. Check with more than one local sign company to see what rules they know about in your area. They may be aware of ordinances that the clerk you talked to at the town hall didn't know about or forgot to tell you about.

Knowing all of the restrictions you have to deal with could actually make your job easier. For example, there's no need to consider a neon sign if the regulations in the Historic District you're in don't allow neon signs.

Your next step should be to drive around town (or even in neighboring towns) and look at other restaurant signs. Do you see any designs you like? Maybe you can talk to the owners and see who designed their signs.

Log onto the Internet and search Google Images for "restaurant sign." Also, go to **www.iStockPhoto.com** and search for the phrase, "restaurant sign." Searching the Internet is a great way to get sign ideas.

When you have an idea of what you want your sign to look like, go to local sign companies and tell them what you want and see what options, advice and prices they can offer. Be sure to go to more than one company.

Don't forget to check out sign companies on the Internet. You could find a better price on the Internet, but keep in mind that there will be shipping and installation costs to factor in and you won't have the advantage of having a local company if repairs or changes need to be made and you most likely won't be able to get local referrals. Checking sign makers in nearby cities is another way to get more options and ideas.

Be sure to include the cost to deliver and install any sign you purchase when comparing the real cost of different signs and different sign companies and proposals. Can you pick up the sign and install it yourself? It could save you money, but in many cases it's worth it to have it installed by someone who knows what they're doing.

Can your old sign be refurbished?

Before you invest a dime in a new sign, take a look at your old sign. Can it be refurbished and/or modified to meet your needs? If it is sturdy and has good "bones," modifying your existing sign and giving it a fresh new look could be your best investment. You would be surprised what new paint and replacing burned out light bulbs can do for a lot of signs that have been neglected for years.

When you know the ordinances and constraints you have to comply with and know the message you want to deliver, you are now ready to meet with sign makers and not be starting with a blank piece of paper.

Here are a five other things to keep in mind about your sign:

1. Bigger is not always better. You don't need a billboard size sign and don't try to fill up all of the space on your sign. Get your basic information across in as few words as possible and with simple graphics.

2. By all means use a type style that is very easy to read. Don't let some graphic designer get carried away with a fancy font that no one can read. Your words and images must be able to be read and understood with just a quick glance.

3. How long is your lease for and do you have an option to renew it? If you think you might choose to (or be forced to) move within a few years, how easy would it be to take your sign with you? These are just things to consider.

4. A sign is extremely valuable to a new restaurant. Don't make the mistake of waiting until all of the renovations are complete and then seeing how much money is left for a sign. There probably won't be any. Get the sign designed and put up early and start creating a buzz. Let people know what type of restaurant is going to be opening. If you have to cut corners, do it somewhere else.

If your restaurant is a 20-year old icon of the community, a sign may not be so important, but for a new restaurant it's vitally important. Hanging a piece of vinyl with stick-on letters out front is not the image you want to portray for your new restaurant.

And one last point. . .

5. The final step: Go back and read the section in Chapter 5 about how to negotiate before you start talking to any company about making a sign for you. After all, when you invest in a sign, you are making a major advertising investment. You can save a **lot** of money with a little negotiating. Remember, there are a many points to negotiate other than the price.

How to Write a Cookbook, Promote Your Restaurant and Put Money in Your Pocket Every Day

A restaurant cookbook can serve as a valuable promotional tool for your restaurant as well as a source of additional revenue.

Can you make a million dollars selling your cookbook? These two women did

Two women in Australia recently published a cookbook and so far have **sold over a million dollars worth** of the books. The cookbook has 340 recipes you can make from just four ingredients. There are no food pictures in the cookbook and the cover is not fancy – not even a photo on the cover of the book. You can do better than that can't you?

To see the million dollar cookbook go to the website below:

www.4ingredients.com.au/

You (or someone on your staff) can design your cookbook and have it ready to print in a few hours.

Below are links to two low-cost ($35 to $50) "Cookbook Designing" software programs you can use to greatly simplify the work.

www.galaxymall.com/foods/cookbookmaker/cbm2000 .html#order

www.cookspalate.com/features.htm

You can search Google for the phrase, "Cookbook Software" and find many more software programs to help you layout and design your cookbook.

Here's how to have your cookbook designed for you for $35 or less

If you want someone to do all the work for you, here's the easy way to have all the work done for you in one day for as little as $35.

www.ScriptLance.com is a web site that matches design projects with creative people from all over the world who are looking to do intellectual work (such as: computer programming, writing, graphic design, web site designs, logo designs, etc.).

You post your project on ScriptLance and get bids from people wanting to do the work. There's no cost to use this service. Don't worry about the project not being done to your satisfaction. You don't pay until you're satisfied with the work.

For example, I posted a project on **www.ScriptLance.com** last week to have a cookbook designed and written including designing the front cover.

In the first five minutes I got bids to do the work that ranged from $35 to $275. The times quoted to do the work ranged from one to seven days.

Over the next three days I received a total of 18 bids that ranged from $30 to $275 with most bids being below $100.

How to post your project on ScriptLance

Below is the way I described the project on ScriptLance. Feel free to use this description (or any modification of it) to describe your own project.

Format a Cookbook. Recipes will be supplied (approximately 60).

Need recipes formatted and put into a Microsoft Word and PDF format so the pages can be printed.

The book will be printed in a spiral binding format. Two pages are to be formatted on an 8 1/2 by 11 page that will be cut in half before assembling.

A basic front and back cover design will be required. Text and graphics or pictures will be supplied.

Job Type:

* Graphic Design * Writing

That's all there is to it. After you post your project on ScriptLance you wait to get the bids, select the person you want to do the work and soon your project will be finished.

You will receive a finished cookbook ready for you to take to Staples for printing (or print on your own printer). You can print a dozen or a hundred copies with the spiral binding that will lay flat when opened.

In addition to having the books printed and spiral bound at Staples or other office supply houses, you can also go to **www.BookSurge.com** and have your books printed one at a time or as many as you want. Paperback books are about $4 to $5 each and if you buy 50 or more, you get a discount. There is a one-time $99 setup fee, but after that you just pay for the number of books you order. They offer books in all the standard sizes. To see an example of their work, this book was printed by BookSurge.

If your cookbook has color pages, you can have pictures and text in color for about $3.15 plus $0.12 per page. There are other options offered like hard covers, etc. You can even have them design your cover for you, but you could probably get a much better price by going to ScriptLance.com.

BookSurge is owned by Amazon.com and they are located in Charleston, SC. You can contact them online at **www.BookSurge.com** or by phone at 1-866-308-6235, Monday through Friday, 9 to 5.

By the way, there are two choices of services that you can use to have the layout and design work done. I used

www.ScriptLance.com because I have used them more, but **www.eLance.com** is a similar service that might be better for this project. Here are my thoughts on when to use which service:

To find writers and graphic designers, go to **www.eLance.com**

To find computer programmers and coders, go to **www.ScriptLance.com**

To see a sample of the kind of cookbooks that are on the market, search Google Images for the word, "Cookbook" and you will find hundreds of examples.

Picture yourself with your own cookbook. Your own cookbook can be on display and be selling in your lobby in less than two weeks.

With your own cookbook, you will be an instant celebrity and your restaurant will be more popular than ever. And don't forget about the extra money you will be making every day for years to come with the sales of your very own cookbook.

Any restaurant with their own cookbook is considered to be a "cut above" the run of the mill restaurants. Why not put your restaurant in this class? What are you waiting for? Who knows, you might be like the two women in Australia who sold over a million dollars worth of their cookbooks in a very short amount of time.

Why stop with writing a cookbook?

Turn the story of your restaurant into a book **and make your restaurant famous**

If you are perceived as knowing more about cooking and preparing your type of food than anyone else in your state or town, you will have a busy restaurant every meal.

The quickest and easiest way to be known as an expert is to. . . Write a book!

It's easier than you think. The title is the most important part of the book. How about,

"Why Mexican food is healthy and good for you"

You can substitute Seafood, Pizza, Southern cooking, Chinese food, BBQ or just about any other type of food in the title.

Here's another title,

"How to cook award winning desserts like a pro"

You can change the word, "desserts" to just about any type of food.

You don't even have to write the book. You can get it done for $100 to $200 at **www.eLance.com** by a ghostwriter.

This $100 to $200 will include researching the topic (let the ghostwriter search the Internet to find out why Mexican food is good for you), designing the cover and writing the whole book.

Just tell them a little about what you know and what you want in the book and they will do the rest of the work for you.

Of course, you would want to proof the book before it was printed and almost surely make a few changes and corrections. You may want to go through the proofing process more than one time.

You can have the books printed a few at a time as was described in the cookbook section.

You can log onto **www.Amazon.com** and go through the steps and have them stock and sell your books also.

Added bonus: Supply a CD with your book and you will really get attention. The CD can just be someone reading the text of the book.

Go to **www.Kunaki.com** and they will produce CDs for you for $1.75 each with no minimum order and no setup charge. (Order one at time if you want to). They will burn the CD and print right on the CD (and even include your restaurant logo on the CD). And they will print the label for the box and shrink wrap the CD and box for you. **All of this for $1.75.**

This one quick project will classify you as an expert for years to come and you will get a lot of publicity from the media and get a lot of customers coming in the door.

Nothing else you will do this year will bring you more customers than this one project. And your total investment is only a couple hundred dollars and three hours of your time.

Technology is wonderful and the restaurant manager who uses it will be the winner in the restaurant marketing race.

## Chapter 13

Home Delivery is No Longer Just for Pizza

Home delivery in the restaurant business is one of the big growth segments. If you don't think home delivery is big business, just look at pizza.

I know you're thinking that you probably can't do enough home delivery business to justify the cost and time to set up a home delivery segment to your business. But here's the easy way to get the benefits of home delivery without any of the overhead, expense and headache.

In almost every city there is at least one business already set up that does home delivery for a few select restaurants. Check your yellow pages to find one (or more) in your area. Do they do delivery for your competitors?

Use their service. Call up and place an order to have food brought to your home. Check to see how the service worked. Were you satisfied? Ask the delivery person which restaurants he or she delivers for the most. Do this two or three times to see what you think about the service.

The advantage of using one of these services is that you get to sell more food. You can set it up so that you don't take orders when your kitchen is too busy to handle extra orders, such as on Friday and Saturday nights or during your busy season if you're in a seasonal resort area.

I did a quick check on the Internet and here are two companies in different parts of the country that do home delivery for local restaurants. Take a look at their websites and see if you think this type of service would benefit your restaurant.

www.takeouttaxi.com/
www.restaurantexpress.com/remenusheader.htm

Of course, check your Yellow Pages and see if the service in your area has a website and if so, be sure to check that out.

The good part about using one of these services is that it costs you nothing to test the concept. And if you can get 10% to 15% of extra business with absolutely no advertising or other costs to you, would it make a big difference to your bottom line?

Home delivery may not be right for your business, but you owe it to yourself to check it out. If you decide to give it a try, you can probably set it up with one phone call and zero risks. The main thing to consider is whether your kitchen has extra capacity or not – if so, setting up home delivery might be a good move for you and your restaurant.

## Chapter 14

How to Use Contests to Prove You're the Best in Your Niche Market

When you win a contest, you can leverage this by putting something about it in all of your ads, fliers, brochures, etc., and it will make any advertising you do much more productive.

Everyone wants to have an enjoyable experience when they go out to eat – whether they go to a fine dining restaurant, or to a fast pizza or BBQ place.

You can say, "we're the BEST" until you're blue in the face and diners will take it with a grain of salt. After all, how many BBQ restaurants do you know of that claim to have the "The world's best BBQ"?

When every restaurant is claiming to be the best, these claims have grown to mean nothing to the general public. The solution is. . . you need someone else to toot your horn and tell the world how great your restaurant is.

There are two ways to do this:

#1. Have stories and reviews in the local media about your restaurant.

#2. Win contests and then quote the results in your ads and promotions.

For example: If you have a seafood restaurant, it would be very convincing if you could say, "Voted Best Seafood Restaurant in Atlanta" or in Maine or wherever. But what if you didn't win in the recent "Reader's Choice Survey," what should you do?

Here are the steps you need to take to promote your restaurant with contests:

1. Take advantage of every opportunity to enter a contest. Enter contests for the best dessert, the best appetizer, the best BBQ ribs, etc.

2. Be a politician and work to turn out the voters any time there's a contest. When the local paper announces a "Reader's Choice" survey, don't just wait to see what happens. This is really a popularity contest. Stack the deck in your favor. Send an email message to everyone on your list asking them to vote for your restaurant. Tell them exactly how to do it – log on this website, or call this phone number or mail in this coupon, etc. Believe me; your competitors are doing it. Mail a letter to everyone on your list that you don't have an email address for.

3. Use your contest wins in all of your advertising. You'd be surprised how many restaurants are voted the best in some category and then never take advantage of this fact in their marketing program. Even if you didn't win "Best Steaks," maybe you did win "best apple pie." However small you think your win is – use it! When you are good at one thing, the public will assume that you are also pretty good at other things, too. This is called the "halo effect."

Winning contests takes effort and commitment, but the payback can yield a great return for your small investment. Put your best efforts into every contest and always be on the lookout for a contest you can enter.

Winning contests can pay big rewards for years to come. Even if you didn't win "Best Pizza" this year, you can still say, "Voted Best Pizza in 2008" Most readers will not even realize that the 2009 contest has already been held.

Place a statement in your ads, email messages and direct mail pieces and say, "voted Best BBQ" (or whatever). Maybe even put a picture of a big blue ribbon next to the statement in your ads. Take these steps and watch your sales go up significantly.

Some final thoughts on contests: Realize they are popularity contests. In any contest more than likely most of the people voting have not eaten at all of the restaurants; therefore, they couldn't really select the best. It would be like judges picking the best ice skater without watching all of the contestants skate. People vote for their favorites, so it really is a popularity contest.

Anytime you are in a contest be sure to send out emails to everyone on your list telling them to vote for your restaurant. Also, tell all of your servers to ask each customer to vote for your restaurant. You can bet that your competition will be doing this. Don't let them win because they were more active than you and your staff.

If you don't win "Best Restaurant," you might win best soup, or best dessert or best BBQ. As long as you win something take advantage of it. If you say you were voted as having the best dessert, people will assume that the rest of the items you serve must be pretty good too. This is what is called the halo effect.

Chapter 15

Good Samaritan Marketing

Nothing beats word-of-mouth advertising, but how do you make it happen?

It's simple. All you need to do is to get someone that people trust and someone who talks to a **lot** of people. Get them to tell all these people about your restaurant.

Get them to tell people what a wonderful time they had at your restaurant and how good your prime rib (or apple pie, or clam chowder, or something was).

(It's very important that they talk about at least one specific thing about your restaurant – an item on the menu, the service, etc. This works much better than just saying everything was wonderful.)

This will quickly drive a crowd to your restaurant, if you get the right person. But who would be the best person to do this and how would you get them to tell dozens and maybe even hundreds of people about your restaurant?

Who fits this position perfectly in every community? – Members of the clergy.

Invite all of the clergy of churches and synagogues within a three to five mile radius of your restaurant in for a completely free meal for two.

You can't get better or cheaper advertising than this. If only one couple comes in one time from the minister's recommendation, you have actually made money.

So unless you really don't have great food and great service, this marketing technique will bring you a lot of customers for absolutely no real cost.

What if you get a dozen or two dozen couples or families and half of them become regular customers?

Of course, don't blow the opportunity. Be sure to give top-notch service and be sure to personally go by and welcome the minister and his wife.

You can mail an invitation to the ministers, but an even better way would be to go visit each one personally and give them a coupon.

Tell them that ministers or priest or rabbis have been good to you and your family and you want to say thank you by inviting them to a free dinner for two at your restaurant. Of course, start by personally going to your clergyman and inviting him and his wife in for a complementary dinner.

Many clergymen will mention their experience Sunday morning in their announcements or welcoming comments before their sermon. They like to talk about upbeat topics when they first start to speak.

Chapter 16

How a $100 Investment in Your Phone System Can Bring You $1,000 a Month of Extra Profit

Wake up the marketing genius inside you. Here's how to make one of the best marketing investments you can ever make.

Did you ever pick up something at a garage sale for almost nothing that was really valuable?

My 87-year-old savvy mother bought a plate at a garage sale for 10¢ recently and sold it on eBay for $114.50. She bought a vase for 50¢ and sold it on eBay for $72.50. What does this have to do with marketing your restaurant? More than you think.

We all like to find bargains. The best way to find a bargain is when other people don't recognize the value of what they have or just want to get rid of it.

For example, one enterprising restaurant owner got the old phone number of a nearby popular restaurant that had gone out of business after 35 years.

He said he gets at least $1,400 a month in sales from the old number and one month his sales resulting directly from the old phone number was over $3,700.

With these numbers and with food costs at about 30% to 35%, this restaurant owner is making an extra $500 to $1,000 a month – month after month – with this one idea.

People call the phone number to get directions or make a reservation at the out-of business restaurant and he has trained his staff to explain that the other restaurant is no longer in business.

With this technique you could say, "Come in to our restaurant tonight and I will give you the best table in the house" or a free dessert or whatever. You can say something like, "We're just half a mile on down the road on the left if you're coming from town."

There are three ways to get the phone numbers of restaurants that have gone out of business

#1. Wait until the phone number becomes available from the phone company. The disadvantage of doing this is that it may not still be available by the time you learn that the phone company has freed it up. The good part about this method of course, is that it's free. If you know of restaurants that went out of business several months ago, call their old number and see if someone has the number. If not, call the phone company and see if it's still available. If an individual has the number, they may be tired of getting calls for the restaurant and be happy to let you have the phone number in exchange for some gift certificates.

#2. Buy the phone number from the owner. When a restaurant goes out of business, it is usually because they ran out of cash. Offer the owner $100 or even $500 if that's what it takes. The example above shows how valuable the phone number could be to you. Or maybe offer him $500 worth of gift certificates to your restaurant.

#3. You have probably negotiated and bought equipment from restaurants that have gone out of business. The next time you do this consider this offer. Say, "I'll give you that much for the equipment if you'll throw in your old phone number."

When you go to see a restaurant owner about buying his old phone number, be sure to take along a copy of the form from the phone company that he has to sign to authorize the transfer. This way the transaction can be completed right then and there.

If he takes time to think about it, he may realize that his old phone number is worth a lot more than what he is selling it to you for.

## Chapter 17

Learn to Make Bad Decisions and Your Restaurant Will Be a Lot More Profitable

Tom Watson, founder of IBM, said that making a bad decision was much better than not making a decision. "If you make a bad decision, you can change it, but if you don't make a decision nothing happens," he said.

In most cases a non-decision costs you more than a bad decision.

As an engineer, I have worked for several R&D departments over the years. Many of them had a policy of giving an award each year for the worst decision of the year. Why did they reward bad decisions?

By letting it be known that bad decisions were acceptable, they were encouraging research engineers and managers to take risks.

The thinking was that if you never make a bad decision, you're being way too cautious. You're missing too many opportunities.

The same thinking works for restaurants, too.

I remember sitting in a marketing class at Harvard Business School many years ago and the professor asked a student what he would do in the restaurant case being discussed. The student made the mistake of saying he would go get more information.

The professor pointed out that this type of thinking was one of the biggest problems of managers – the failure to make decisions. You can keep getting more information until your restaurant is out of business. To be successful you have to make decisions, he said.

The Harvard professor said, "Every business decision is made with incomplete information."

If you're like most managers, you fail to make way too many decisions. When you fail to make a decision, you really are making a decision.

Let your managers know that it's okay to make some bad decisions, and then you'll see a lot more innovation and profit making opportunities being implemented.

Here's an example of what I mean about not making a decision.

I was consulting with a restaurant owner recently on his advertising. Over a period of several weeks he reviewed a $295 ad proposal 12 times and never made a decision. (Yes, the salesman made 12 trips back to see him.) I couldn't help but wonder what he would do if a big decision came along.

Of course, you have to be cautious and not make too many bad decisions, but you may be missing a lot of opportunities by not making decisions.

Bottom line: Follow Tom Watson's example and make decisions and then change the decision if the facts change or if different information becomes available. This technique made Tom Watson a lot of money. It'll work for you too.

## Chapter 18

Be a Server in Your Own Restaurant and You'll Make More than Just Tips

Here's a marketing technique used by the owner of one of the top-100 restaurants in the country. It doesn't cost you a dime to implement this technique and, in addition to bringing in customers, it puts cash in your pocket every time you use it.

Is there really such a marketing technique?

I sat down with the owner of one of the top 100 up-scale restaurants in the country last week and found out a simple marketing technique he uses to increase sales for his restaurant.

Of all the advertising and analysis he does, this simple no-cost technique makes him more money than anything else – and it really does put cash in his pocket.

What does he do?

It's simple. At least one evening a week he works as a waiter in his own restaurant.

Here are the advantages:

1. It really builds customer loyalty. The regulars love to see him and even if he's not waiting on their table, they speak to him and know he's on top of things. Everyone likes to feel as though he knows the owner.

2. He learns a lot about what's going on in his restaurant. Is the kitchen running behind? Are the tables being bused fast enough? Is the music too loud?

3. It builds employee loyalty. In staff meetings he has firsthand experience with employee problems and concerns. He experiences the same problems they experience.

4. He gets real-time feedback on the food quality and general customer satisfaction.

He said that he could hire a consultant and wouldn't get nearly as much real information about his restaurant as he gets from working one night a week as a waiter.

"Repeat customers are where the real profit is for most restaurants and this technique is one of the best ways I've seen to build loyalty and bring customers back," he said.

Try it. It doesn't cost anything and, as the successful restaurant owner who uses it said, at the end of the night you'll even have tip money in your pocket.

## Chapter 19

How to Redesign Your Menu and Reap Huge Rewards

You have invested a lot of money to get someone into your restaurant. Now when you hand them a menu you have 109 seconds (according to a Gallup study) to convince them to spend more money and to spend it on the items that give you the most profit. Look at the numbers:

If your restaurant sales average $1.5 million a year and you can increase the average profit on each dollar of sales by 5%, that means $75,000 of extra profit a year will fall straight to the bottom line and if you could get 10% extra profit, it would give you an extra $150,000.

If football is a game of inches, then the restaurant business is surely a game of pennies. You can do a lot of menu analysis and tweaking for $75,000 to $150,000 of extra profit a year.

It's not as simple as just raising your prices. There is this thing economists call, "price-elasticity" of demand. If the price-elasticity of an item is not very much, a price increase or decrease will not affect the amount sold very much.

For example, if the price of a box of table salt doubled, would you decrease the quantity of table salt you purchased? In fact, you probably wouldn't change your buying habits of table salt if the price went up by a factor of 10. For example if the price of salt went from $0.59 a box to $5.90 a box, you probably wouldn't cut back on your use of salt.

Unfortunately, items on your menu are very inelastic. That means that a small change in price one way or the other can have a huge effect on the quantity sold. You can add value, by giving the item a sexy or catchy name or add a special sauce, etc. This might allow you to make a larger change in the price because of the difference in perceived value, but in most cases you are stuck with tweaking and making minor price changes. Be sure to make them slowly.

Forget about cost-plus pricing. The price your customers are willing to pay for an item is based on perceived value and the alternatives (if steak gets too expensive, they will select chicken). What an item costs you to prepare has absolutely nothing to do with what a customer is willing to pay for the item.

The perceived value is based not just on the quality of the food and the service, but on the atmosphere and décor of your restaurant as well as whether you offer a great view or have live entertainment, etc. All of this adds to the enjoyment of the meal and, therefore, to the price you can charge. And of course, what your competitors are charging will factor into what a customer is willing to pay you for an item, also.

When setting or adjusting your prices, first decide what your boundaries are – the minimum you can sell an item for and still make an acceptable profit and the maximum the market will bear based on your competition and the alternatives. Then decide on your prices with these two end points in mind. If a competitor is drastically under-pricing you on an item, don't try to match his price and lose money. He may be losing money on the item and just doesn't know it yet. Hold your price or take the item off the menu.

After you do your research and analysis of your prices, don't ignore your gut feel. If you think a price is too high and you wouldn't pay that much, go with your gut.

One point to remember is to **never make wholesale, across the menu price increases**. Your customers will notice this and may not come back. Make small changes to only a few items at a time.

To adjust your prices for maximum profitability, start by looking at the numbers as outlined below.

Your menu should be divided into categories: seafood, steaks, sandwiches, appetizers, desserts, salads, etc. with a maximum of five to six items in a category. (If your items are not grouped this way on your menu now, group the items into categories for this analysis.)

The first step is to get an accurate cost of each item in the category and the percentage of sales each item in the category represents compared to the whole category. Then construct a simple graph with the percent of sales on the vertical axis and gross profit on the horizontal axis.

Then place a dot on the graph for each item in the category. Now draw a horizontal line and a vertical line on the graph dividing the graph roughly into four quadrants and label the four quadrants 1, 2, 3 and 4 with 1 being the bottom left quadrant, 2 being the bottom right quadrant, 3 being the top left quadrant and 4 being the top right quadrant as shown below.

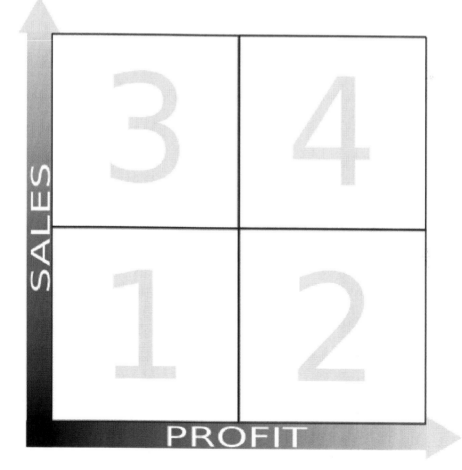

What you want to do is find your winners and your "dogs" in the category. Here is a description of the four categories:

Category 1: Low sales volume and low profit per sale. These are your "dogs." You don't sell many of these items and you don't make much when you do.

Category 2: These are high profit items, but you don't sell many of them, so your total revenue for this category is low even though you are making a high profit on the items when you do sell them.

Category 3: You sell a lot of these items, but don't make much on each sale. Therefore, low total revenue from the category.

Category 4: These are your winners. You sell a lot of these items and you make a high profit on each item. You would like for all of your items to move towards this category.

Now, let's talk about what you should do with the items in each of the weaker categories. Your first thought might be to eliminate all of the "dog" items in Category 1. I'm sure you can and should eliminate some of them, but some of the items might have to stay on the menu such as kids' meals, vegetarian items, etc. because you'll lose other customers if you don't carry them. Also, you can consider raising the price of some of the items. If they don't sell at the higher price, you haven't lost much, because you weren't selling enough of the items to matter anyway.

Category 2 items have a lot of potential. Your profit is high. You just need to sell more of the items. We will talk about how to do this later when we talk about where and how to place items on the menu.

Category 3 items are selling well, but you are not making much profit on the items. Consider making small price increases on these items and continue increasing the price gradually over time until you start to see a decrease in sales volume.

Of course, another way to make items in Category 3 more profitable other than raising the price is to decrease the cost. Can this be done without losing the quality or appeal?

You can also add a picture for even more emphasis, but be sure to use a high-quality picture. Use a professional food photographer or go to www.iStockPhoto.com and get high-quality stock photos for $2 to $5 each and you will have rights to use of the pictures.

Here are some guidelines on designing your menus

By all means **don't have the background behind the text anything except white or yellow**. Colors or designs in the background make the menu hard to read. I was at a restaurant not long ago that had very light small black print on a dark red menu and in the low light of the restaurant it was impossible for me to read a single word on the menu.

DON'T USE ALL CAPS LIKE THIS IN YOUR ITEMS DESCRIPTIONS. As you can see, the all caps text is very hard to read. Instead of drawing attention, it makes the reader skip reading it.

Make all of your prices end with a "9." If you have prices that end with ".95" change them all to ".99." Your sales will not suffer at all and the pennies will add up.

Don't use the phrase, "Market Price." What this says to the customer is that the item is **very** expensive. A better way to do it is to list the highest expected price and then have the item "on special" at a lower price any time you are not charging the highest price.

For example, you could list Lobster on the menu at $21.95 and then have it on special tonight for $17.95 and it will seem like a real bargain. Of course, it may end up being on special most of the life of that particular menu, but you will sell a lot more of the item using this technique than you will if you listed the price as "Market Price."

Don't right justify your prices. Place the prices at the end of the description where they naturally fall. If you line the prices up along the right margin, a customer can scan down the list and select the lowest price item.

Don't give your graphic designer a free hand when it comes to laying out your menu. Many graphic designers will make the menu fancy, but it will be hard to read.

Don't use laminated menus. They are expensive and you will be tempted to not make changes as often as you should because of the expense you will incur. A good choice for your menu is to use good quality plastic covers with paper inserts. Search Google for "menu covers" and you will find a lot of vendors and options to choose from.

Don't make your menus too large. Large menus can knock over wine glasses and keep the guests from seeing and conversing with other members of their party. This is especially true for small tables. A size of 9" by 12" is a good choice because it will accommodate 8½ x 11" paper inserts.

If your menu starts to get too large, don't be tempted to use small print or a lot of pages, consider having a separate wine menu, separate kids' menu and separate dessert menu. In most cases a separate dessert menu with pictures (or a dessert tray) will greatly increase the sale of dessert items anyway.

If you have room on the back of your menu, **tell your story** – why your restaurant is special – you wash the vegetables three times, you make your own bread and your own salad dressings, you use old family recipes, you have an award winning chef, your great grandfather started the restaurant, etc.

You can get software templates especially for menus which include icons, pictures and formats, or your paper supplier can supply you with pre-printed themed menu paper (or search Google for suppliers), but don't go with fancy background designs. Having fancy themed designs around the text and inserting graphics and pictures in and around the category boxes is fine, but do not have your text printed on top of anything except a white or yellow background (you can use different shades of yellow for variety).

Color printers are inexpensive now. Printing your own menus and menu inserts quickly in-house gives you great flexibility in tweaking the price of items and changing the emphasis given to items to maximize your profit.

Be sure to have the name of your restaurant, your address, phone number, hours of operation and your website domain name on your menus. Sometimes people take a menu as a souvenir or they want to show it to a friend. If they do, you at least want them to know which restaurant the menu came from and how to find you so they can come back.

Keep in mind that the things you can control and adjust to make your menu more profitable are the price you charge, the placement of the item on the menu, the presentation (picture of the food) and the promotion of an item.

In summary, to maximize your profit, determine your most profitable and popular items and place them on the menu in a way so they will be seen and therefore ordered more often. This means placing them in the first or second position in the category box or the last position.

For example, put your three most profitable seafood items in the first, second and last position in the seafood category on your menu. Items in these three positions will be seen more and, therefore, ordered more often. This is one of the best ways to sell more of your high profit items.

By all means place all categories in separate boxes or in separate areas on your menu.

Tweak prices in small increments and on only a few items at a time to determine the "sweet" spot to maximize your overall profit. Be sure to track the results as you make changes to the menu.

One last point – **clone your winners**. For example, if shrimp scampi is a winner, try other shrimp dishes. Take a look at your winners and see if there is a way to clone them.

## Chapter 20

How to Market to Tourists

According to National Restaurant Association research, travelers and visitors account for roughly 30 percent of the sales at fine dining restaurants and approximately 20 percent of the sales at family and casual-dining restaurants.

Of course, in a tourist area, the percentages would be larger and they would be smaller in a very non-tourist area. But everywhere is becoming a tourist area. A lot of people want to go where the tourists don't go, but that's getting to be almost impossible as you will see from the examples below.

My brother and his wife spent the summer traveling from Florida to Washington State and back and their goal was to see the non-tourist areas of the country. They took the back roads and went through small towns and out of the way places. They were surprised to see other tourists everywhere they went.

I spent two months recently in Costa Rica in the non-tourist, rainy season. I spent a lot of the time traveling to remote areas and visiting very small towns. I was surprised that in almost every restaurant I sat down in I would see other tourists there, also.

Tourists are everywhere and to be successful in the restaurant business, you can't ignore the tourist business regardless of where you're located.

Are you getting your fair share of this market? The heck with getting your fair share, why not go after way more than just your "fair" share of this market? This chapter is going to show you how to do just that.

We all know that when we go on vacation, a weekend get-away, or even on a business trip, dining out at some of the local and unique restaurants is one of the most enjoyable parts of the trip and a big part of what we look forward to.

To capture the tourist market, one of the things you have to do is to become a tourist attraction. The best part about doing what it takes to attract tourists is that it also attracts a lot of locals. If your restaurant captures the flair, image and essence of your area with food, décor and ambiance, you will become the one restaurant where locals will want to bring their out of town guests. As an added bonus, you will capture the attention of the local and national newspaper and travel writers. They are always looking for interesting places to write about. Their stories will give you great publicity and a lot of business.

Here's what you want people to be saying about your restaurant: "While you're in Mayberry be sure to eat at the Old Mill Steakhouse" or "While you're here, we have to take you to Jenny's Bistro." That's what you want previous visitors and locals to be saying about your restaurant.

When people are away from home they want to experience something that is unique and local – something they can't get at home.

To capture more than your share of the tourist market in your area, there are only two things you have do:

#1. Become a tourist attraction.

#2. Let the world know that you are, "The place to eat and the place to see when in [your area]."

Here's how you accomplish both of those things.

To become a tourist attraction, the first thing you have to do is give tourists a taste of your local cuisine, flair or history – do this with the types of food you serve, the names you give to your menu items and how your restaurant is decorated.

The way to give tourists a taste of your regional specialties is to feature local dishes, of course. For example, if you are in the South you could feature local favorites such as turnip greens, fried green tomatoes, shrimp and grits, etc. in additional to your traditional steaks, salmon, etc. – and be sure to give even your traditional dishes colorful names – Uncle Jake's T-Bone Steak or Aunt Bessie's apple pie.

Whether it's catfish, crab cakes, chili, grilled buffalo steaks country fried chicken, or at least crawfish, there are regional specialties that are not common in other parts of the country and they are not prepared the way they're prepared in your area. For example, even BBQ is fixed different ways in different parts of the country.

Of course, the name you give your menu items can add a lot to the theme. Don't just have buffalo wings on your menu, have California style buffalo wings or Uncle Henry's buffalo wings.

Capture local flair and culture with the theme and decorations of your restaurant. Decorate at least one dining room (or even one section of a dining room) in a way that highlights local history or customs. All you have to do is a little more than the other restaurants in town.

The next step is to let the world know that your restaurant really is "the place to go" to capture the local flavor and flair of the area.

Five things you can do to drive a herd of tourists to your restaurant

#1. Have an Internet presence.

A lot of people search for restaurants on the Internet before they visit an area. Go back and review the chapter on "Internet Marketing" and, of course, be sure to implement the Internet marketing techniques outlined in that chapter. When someone searches Google for restaurants in your city, you want to be at the top of the list. You can be with a little effort.

#2. Join your local Chamber of Commerce and your local Convention and Visitors Bureau.

Get information from them about upcoming conventions and groups planning to visit your area. Send menus and brochures to the groups way ahead of the scheduled trip. When you join the Chamber of Commerce, be sure to get them to link to your website.

#3. Advertise in the local tourist attraction publications.

In most cases media advertising is not cost effective, but this could be an exception. But be sure to track the cost and the results of <u>all</u> of your tourist marketing efforts – you will quickly find out what's working and what's not working.

Don't just throw money at the project and advertise in all of the "Where To Go" tourist type publications just because that's what all of the other restaurants are doing.

If you're in a tourist area, there are sure to be some tourist publications like, "Where to Go," What to Do," "Local Scene" or similar names. These are free publications that are given out everywhere and most tourists are sure to pick up one. As we have discussed before, print advertising in newspapers is usually not a good advertising investment except in a few situations, but advertising in a tourist publication in a tourist area usually does pay off.

If there is only one such publication in your area, that's good. If there are two publications, chances are that tourists are going to pick up both of them. Advertising in both of the publications won't give you twice as much business, but it may still pay off to advertise in both publications – you have to test and track the results.

As in all print media publications, try to get your ad on the right hand page even if you have to pay a little extra. The top right corner is the best place if it's not too expensive. If you can get the top right corner for 10% to 20% extra, take it.

#4. Bed and breakfast guests are a gold mine for savvy restaurant marketers.

B&B owners are asked every night by almost all of their guests, "Where is a good place to go eat?"

B&Bs are different from hotels because B&B guests form a lot closer bond with the owner or manager. Guests ask for and trust the advice from B&B owners a **lot** more than they do hotel managers. There are not as many guests at a B&B as there are at hotels, but you may find that you can get more business from a B&B than you can from a hotel.

Every person staying in a bed and breakfast is going to go out to eat dinner somewhere – and maybe even lunch the next day. You want to make sure that a large percentage of them come to your restaurant.

Bed and breakfast guests want a nice meal and a great experience – and they're willing to pay above average to get it. If they were not looking for a great experience, they wouldn't be staying in a B&B in the first place. This is the kind of customers you want.

You can deliver the experience they're looking for. And when you do deliver this wonderful experience, it makes their enjoyment of their stay at the Bed and Breakfast that much better. You and the B&B owner both win!

Your assignment this week is to contact every bed and breakfast owner within 10 miles of your restaurant and make them an offer they can't refuse.

Here's the offer you make – invite the owner and their spouse or friend to dine in your restaurant as your guests – complete with desserts and a bottle of wine.

After they enjoy the wonderful experience you can deliver, tell them that you can deliver this same experience to their guests and that you will give the bed and breakfast owner a credit of 10% of the total amount of the checks for every customer they send you. The B&B owners or managers can use this credit to dine in your restaurant.

Point out to them how much they would earn if they only sent one couple a night to your restaurant – probably enough to dine out every week.

Here's how to implement this bed and breakfast program.

Leave the B&B owners a stack of your brochures and your personal business cards with a handwritten note on the back saying, "Free appetizer for guests of "Mountain View Bed and Breakfast with this card."

The B&B owners will make sure that they (or their staff) recommend your restaurant to everyone who asks about where to eat – and probably to a lot of people who don't ask. Of course, be sure to keep the cards and record the total amount of the check so you can reward the B&B owners.

This one simple technique can easily add $1,000 a month to your bottom line profits for every bed and breakfast that's within 10 miles of your restaurant.

#5. Grab the tourists in nearby hotels and motels.

Most people staying in hotels and motels are going to eat at least one meal (and maybe eat two or three meals) somewhere near where they're staying. You want your share (or more than your share) of this business. Don't let the starving tourists in motels and hotels within sight of your restaurant go somewhere else to eat.

Consider arranging a free shuttle (provided by your restaurant or the hotel) between your restaurant and the nearby hotels. Start this service with a few hotels and expand it if it pays off.

The three best ways to get business from the hotels and motels are to:

- Have the front desk highly recommend your restaurant.
- Have information about your restaurant actually in the rooms.
- Have brochures and fliers on the front counter and on tables.

I was out of town doing some consulting for a few days last week. As I was checking into a motel, I noticed some fliers on the front counter. The fliers were from a restaurant across the street from the motel.

I asked the lady at the front desk if it was a good place to eat and she said, "I don't know. I've never eaten there." Are front desk staff members at nearby hotels and motels saying the same thing about your restaurant?

Follow through on your marketing efforts

The restaurant owner in the above example had taken the first step to get guests of the motel to know about his restaurant, but I wonder how much more business he could get if he would take the next step and treat each of the front desk staff to a FREE dinner (along with a spouse or friend, of course)?

I know the front desk staff changes a lot and there are several members of the staff, but feeding them even once every three months could be one of the most productive and the lowest-cost marketing techniques you could use. At the very least, find out who is working during the late afternoon and early evening hours and treat these people to a free meal one time to see how much business it generates for you.

In addition to having the front desk staff recommending your restaurant, you will get even more business if you have information about your restaurant in every hotel/motel room. A lot of people make a decision about where to eat while they are in their room and they don't ask the front desk staff.

How to get information about your restaurant in every hotel and motel room in your area.

First, let me tell you how the system works. Almost every hotel and motel chain requires what is called an "in-room directory" book to be in every room. The chains require this book in the room with all of the basic information about the hotel/motel (such as where the ice machines are located, when is checkout time, etc.) In fact, the hotels and motels get penalized if they don't have these in-room directories in the rooms when corporate does their inspections.

The hotels and motels usually contract with a company to produce the books for them. The companies produce the books free in exchange for getting to sell ads to go in the books. If the hotel/motel is in an area where there are not many restaurants, then the company producing the books will not be able to sell enough ads to cover their costs and make a profit and then the hotel/motel will have to pay to have the books printed.

It's usually a worthwhile investment to have your ad in these in-room directories for the hotels and motels that are nearby – IF you can get your ad in the book for a good price. The price you have to pay to get your ad in these directories is very, very negotiable. Go back and read the negotiating section of this book before dealing with the ad salesperson.

There are three problems when it comes to getting your ad in the books.

- The ad rep may not even come by your restaurant to see you. (Ad sales people many times do a hap-hazard job of selling ads.)

- The books are usually produced once a year and if the books have just been produced, it may be another year or more before you would normally have a chance to get your ad in the directories.

- With the economy being slow, the in-room directories for many hotels and motels are not being updated every year. I have seen a lot hotels and motels that have directories in the rooms that are three or four years old. So it could be a few years before you could get your ad in the directories if you just waited for an ad salesperson to contact you.

- You need to take the bull by the horns and make things happen if you want to get information about your restaurant in these in-room directories.

To make this happen, start by visiting each nearby hotel and motel in your area. Do this between 9:00 AM. and 1:00 PM while the rooms are being cleaned. Don't start at the front desk. Start by walking by an open door while the rooms are being cleaned and ask the maid if you can check the in-room directory book. They will always let you.

Take a look to see what kind of books, directories, and fliers are in the room. Most hotels will have an in-room directory. Their in-room directory will either be in the form of a loose-leaf notebook or a stapled and folded booklet. You want to have this "research" information before you contact the manager so you will know what to propose to him or her.

Now your next step is to go by and introduce yourself to the general manager. While you're talking to the manager invite him or her and their guest to have dinner at your restaurant, complete with wine, dessert and the works - complementary of course. Maybe offer the same complementary meal to the front desk manager, also.

Ask the manager if you could place your preprinted sheets in the in-room directories. Tell him you will pay him for the time and effort involved. Also ask to place menus, brochures and fliers in the lobby. You can almost always get your information in the rooms if you follow the above steps.

(Note: You can print one-page color sheets on 60-lb cover stock paper to go in the loose leaf books or to stand up in the plastic holders that are on the desk or table holding all of the other hotel information if they don't have loose leaf binder type in-room directories.)

Following the above steps will get your ads in the hotel and motel rooms immediately and a year or so from now, when a company is updating the books, they will see your ad and be sure to contact you about putting your ad in the upcoming edition of the directories. This way your information will be in the directories immediately and you won't miss out on getting your ad in upcoming editions.

By the way, when and if a company does contact you about putting your information in the new directories cut a deal to leave your ad in the book that is already there and print a few extra sheets to give them for the extra books that will be needed to replace the ones that get lost or stolen each year. You should be able to cut a good deal this way, because the company printing the directories won't incur any cost to place your ad in the books.

All of the above information is talking about what to do when there are loose leaf notebook type directories in the rooms. If there are folded and stapled booklets in the rooms, you will want to negotiate with the hotel/motel manager to place your brochures in the room (and maybe even inside the existing directory books.

Go by the hotel in person from time to time and personally thank the manager and the front desk staff. This will do a lot to get you additional business. As an added bonus, if you can call the front desk staff by name when you go in, that will really help get you business.

Make use of the racks for brochures at the front entrance of hotels and motels – if the price is right. You can't just place your brochure in the rack, you have to pay the person who owns and manages the space. Contact that person and get the information. This can be a good investment, but sometimes they will be putting racks in 50 or so hotels in a 25 mile radius. See if you can contract to just put brochures in the hotels near your restaurant – if you can't, it's probably not worth it to pay to have your brochures placed in such a large radius.

By all means, negotiate to have your brochure near the top of the rack. Also contract for a short period - only one month if possible and track the results. If you have your information in every room of the hotel, the brochure rack in the lobby will not be as valuable to you. Be sure to track the results during your one month test and see if it's paying off. Also be sure to check to make sure your brochures are actually placed in the racks and in the position you negotiated for.

Here's one final thought on marketing to tourists. The efforts you expend to attract tourists pays off for years to come. When a tourist comes to your restaurant and has a wonderful and enjoyable experience, they will tell a lot of people and they will be back. It may be next year before you see them again, but they will be back.

What are you waiting for? Start implementing the steps now to make your restaurant a tourist attraction and get more than your fair share of the tourist business in your area and as an added bonus, you will attract a lot more of the locals, too.

## Chapter 21

What Are Your Competitors Up To?

What are their weaknesses and strong points?

This chapter is near the end of the book, but maybe it should be one of the first things you should do – Find out what your competitors are up to. Is their business for sale? Are they doing everything right? Are they doing anything right? Are they making their customers happy? What are their weaknesses?

Here are two things you should do on a regular basis to keep abreast of your market and your competitors.

The first thing you need to do to is to check the Internet monthly to see which restaurants in your area are for sale. Search Google for the phrase, "Businesses for sale" or "Restaurants for sale" and you will find several websites with the information you want. Below are three sites I refer to for this information:

www.restaurants-for-sale.com/

www.BizBuySell.com

www.businessbroker.net/

You don't want to copy the techniques of restaurants that are going out of business.

The next thing you should do is to dine at your competitors' restaurants often. In addition to you taking a look at your competitors, it's a good idea to have some of your trusted waiters, waitresses and staff check things out for you, too. After all, when you dine there, you might be treated special and not get the regular treatment an ordinary customer would receive.

Tell them to go out to eat with a friend and bring you the check and you will reimburse them for the cost of the dinner. They will enjoy getting to take a friend out to eat and will be happy that you selected them to do it. Keep it low key. There's no need to broadcast to the world what you're doing.

Maybe you could offer the free dinner at a competitor's restaurant as the monthly prize for the waiter or waitress who collected the most birthday/database forms for the month. This way you could get two birds with one stone.

Their first impressions and initial gut feel are important, but it's also important to have a structured form for them to fill out for you. (Of course, tell them **not** to fill out the form while they're at the restaurant. You don't want them to look like they're gathering information.)

Photocopy and print out the form below (or type up your own form) and have your staff use it when evaluating restaurants. It's short, simple and gives you the information you need.

Use this form to identify and copy the good things the other restaurants are doing and also use it to point out their weaknesses so you can take advantage of them. Add or delete anything you want in order to customize the form to fit your needs.

When you go over the form, note the use of the word, "our" in the form. This helps make your employees feel special and valued.

Competitor Evaluation Form

Name of Restaurant being evaluated:

_____

Name of person doing the evaluation:

_____

Date: _____ What time did you walk in?

_____

Did you have to wait? _____ and if so how long? _____
How close was your wait time compared to what they told you?

_____

What percent of their tables were full when you arrived? _____ When you left? _____

On a scale of 1 to 10 (with 5 being about average, 1 being the worse you have ever seen and 10 being the best you have ever seen), rate the following things: (Note: If it doesn't apply or you don't remember, leave the item blank.) Add comments with additional information where applicable.

_____ Overall first impression

_____ Parking

_____ How long did you have to wait to get a table?

_____ After you ordered how long did it take to get your food?

_____ Cleanliness of Restrooms

_____ Friendliness of staff

_____ How was the quality of the food? What did you have?
_____ What did your friend have?

_____

Other comments about the food if any:

_____

_____ Noise level

_____ How well did they handle special requests?

_____ Accuracy of your order

_____ Cleanliness and maintenance of the restaurant

_____ Entertainment? What kind and how was it?

_____

_____ Prices

_____ Atmosphere of the restaurant

Overall, how does this restaurant compare to ours?

_____

What three things does this restaurant do that our restaurant doesn't do or doesn't do as well as this restaurant? In other words, what three ideas should we consider copying and implement?

1.

2.

3.

Misc. comments: Was there anything you observed (good or bad) that was not covered on this form?

_____

_____

_____

_____

_____

_____

## Chapter 22

How to Book Catering Events and Private Parties

Operating a catering business and hosting private parties are really two separate profit centers with different pros and cons. Maybe each of these opportunities or profit centers should be discussed in its own chapter, but I decided to combine them in the same chapter because this book is about how to market your restaurant and these two opportunities are **marketed** pretty much the same way.

Before we go into the marketing, let's stop and take a quick look at whether you should start doing both or just one and if only one, which one. I will go over the details of both of these options to help you decide what you should do.

Let's start by discussing the pros and cons of going into hosting private parties and banquets.

Private parties, banquets and special events

To simplify things I will lump private parties, banquets and special events into one group and refer to all three of them as private parties.

Hosting private parties can be a big boost or it can spell disaster for your restaurant. The key is whether you have extra dining room space or not. Private parties usually tie up the room being used for the entire evening (or entire mealtime in the case of breakfast or lunch meetings). If you could use this area to have two or three table-turns during the same time period the private party is being held, you may lose a lot of revenue during this time slot.

So bottom line, if you have a room that's unused most of the time or a larger dining room than your regular business can make use of, you need to seriously consider private parties. Of course, if you don't have the unused facilities, booking the private parties could actually cost you money.

Catering

One big advantage of the catering business over hosting private parties is that the catering business is scalable. You can easily increase it to whatever size your marketing can support. You can quickly hire more staff. You can add additional kitchen space in non-prime locations and you can quickly rent the extra equipment you need without tying up or risking a lot of capital. You can even rent delivery vans and put your magnetic signs on the outside of the vans and look very professional and also get free advertising while you're driving around town.

Catering is a great way to increase your restaurant's revenue. One of the biggest advantages is that every time you cater an event you get to advertise your restaurant. At any event everyone always knows who did the catering and a lot of people will get to sample your food who have never been to your restaurant and maybe never even heard of your restaurant. In addition to being profitable on its own, catering can bring a lot of new customers into your restaurant – and with zero advertising cost.

But everything about catering is not rosy. You have to consider some of the cons before you jump into catering.

Catering can distract and overburden your already overloaded staff. Can your manager handle the extra time-consuming duties? Can your chef, kitchen staff and space handle the extra volume? Who is going to handle the marketing? You (or someone) will usually have to meet with the person hosting the event and you will probably have to meet with them more than one time. . . and you still might not get their business.

There are some housekeeping jobs that you will need to take care of before you go into the catering and private parties business. You will need contracts (with cancellation penalties spelled out, hold harmless liabilities clauses, etc.). You will want your attorney to prepare the contracts.

Before going into the catering business, do your homework. What are your competitors offering and charging? Can you compete with what they're offering? Get a friend who has a business to contact the different restaurants in the area that offer catering and are hosting private parties. Get copies of their presentation materials and their prices. Also, check with companies that do catering and don't operate a restaurant. Get their information.

Now let's talk about how to market private parties and catering events. This information could even help you in your decision about whether or not to go into these businesses. After all, you don't want to go into these businesses and not have any customers and not know how to get any.

How to book catering and private parties on a shoestring budget

Below are the proven best marketing techniques ever used to book catering and private parties. And the best part is that these techniques will cost you almost nothing and can bring in a ton of business.

1. **Use table tents.** This is one of the best and lowest cost ways to let your customers know that you offer catering services and that you host private parties. Your present customers are the best place to look for catering and private party clients.

2. **Put up discrete framed signs in the lobby** (or large banners depending on the style of your restaurant) saying that you offer these services. Maybe even include some urgency and a call to action by saying, "Holiday dates are booking fast. Talk to a manager tonight to lock in your date."

3. **Put signs in your restrooms** – behind the urinals and on the inside of the doors in the stalls.

4. **Use your website.** Put a prominent note on the Home page of your website saying that you do catering and host

private parties. Later as you develop this part of your business, you can make the note a clickable link that goes to a page that gives more information, menus, pricing, etc.

5. **Include a note in your email message** announcing that you have started doing catering and hosting private parties. Maybe even include this information as the bottom line of every email message from now on.

6. **Put inserts in your menus** and maybe add a line at the bottom of each menu page the next time you print your menus.

7. **Change the on-hold message on your telephone system to announce that you now do catering and host private parties.** Point out that you can cater or host private parties for any size group from two up to 100 (or whatever number you can handle).

8. **Consider doing direct mail to the businesses in your area.** Tell them that you specialize in hosting business meetings for businesses in the Forest Lake area (or whatever your local area is called). It works great when you emphasize that you specialize in working with businesses in the local area and actually name the area.

9. **Be aware of and go after the most profitable types of events** such as: wedding receptions, bar mitzvahs, graduations, retirement parties, civic functions, business meetings, sales meetings, etc.

10. **Contact civic organizations** in your area with the same message.

11. **Consider hosting private parties and events for breakfast and lunch meetings** and not just events in the evenings.

12. **Contact the receptionists in all of the doctors' offices in your area and get the names of all of the pharmacy reps who call on them.** Leave the receptionist a stack of your brochures and cards and tell her to have the pharmacy reps contact you and you will cater some great meals for the office. Of course, if you get the names of the pharmacy reps, you can contact them

yourself. These guys have big budgets to feed the doctors and their staff. You want your part of these large budgets. Of course, they will try to beat you down on the price, so be prepared to negotiate and walk away if you have to.

13. **The best way to close a sale is to have a professional looking presentation package** – maybe even a nice folder embossed with your restaurant name. Include sheets inside the folder with sample menus and pricing. Also, list any special equipment you provide such as, A/V equipment, wireless microphones, DVD player and large screen TV, etc. A professional looking presentation package will go a long way towards closing the sale.

14. **Provide three pricing levels** – low, medium and high end and show the menu item options in each price range. Make it easy for the host to say, "Yes" to your offer with the least amount of time, effort and the fewest decisions required on their part. Don't ask them to come up with a menu.

15. After you get all the easy business using the techniques described above, you can go after the harder to get business by **hiring a full-time or part-time person to market your services**. Pay them on a commission basis and you will get their best efforts and you will have minimum risk.

Now you know how to market catering and private parties. Run these profit centers right and you can add a lot of profit to your bottom line. As an added bonus, these events will bring in many extra customers for your restaurant.

As was stated before, a lot of people will get a chance to taste your food who have never been in your restaurant or maybe never even heard of your restaurant. You will get a lot of free advertising from these endeavors.

Do your homework and see if you should add catering and private parties as a profit center for your restaurant.

## Chapter 23

It's Never Too Late to Have a Grand Opening

A grand opening is not just for new restaurants. Older established restaurants can make a big profit from a grand opening IF the grand opening is done right. they can jump start their restaurants and create the momentum to keep the profits rolling in. Here's how.

One of the main reasons to have a grand opening is to get the news media's attention and then use that media attention to drive a huge crowd to your restaurant.

But how do you have a grand opening for an established restaurant that has been in business for years?

There are three things you need in order to have a really successful, profit-producing grand opening for an established restaurant.

#1. Announce a "reason why" you're having a grand opening. Facts tell, but stories sell. You need a story to explain why you're having a grand opening.

Below are some sample headlines showing you what other successful restaurants have used as their "reason why."

"21 years ago when we opened our restaurant, we were so busy, we forgot to have a grand opening – so we're having one now"

(Of course, if you did have a grand opening when you opened, you can always say, "We didn't have a **proper** grand opening.")

or

"We're having a grand opening to celebrate our three year anniversary"

or

"The Rusty Nail Restaurant has been totally remodeled and we're inviting you to our grand opening to help us celebrate"

#2. Then create a real news-worthy event. The news media love to report on EVENTS.

So all you have to do is to create an event and the news media will love you – and most important – they will tell the world about you and your event.

One of the easiest ways to create an event is to have a grand opening, but you can't just "say" you are going to have a grand opening – you have to actually create a REAL, exciting event.

Seven things that will help make your grand opening a real newsworthy event

You don't need to do all seven of these things to have a successful grand opening. And I'm sure you can think of a few even better things to do that will get your customers and potential customers excited, but these items will give you some ideas.

Which ones and how many you include will depend on your location, market, budget, etc., but the more of these you include, the more newsworthy your grand opening will be and, therefore, the more news coverage you will get.

1. **Have live music** – or better yet, have a contest with several bands or several musicians competing. This gets more media attention and you don't have to pay musicians who are competing in a contest.

2. **Have a hot air balloon**.

3. **Have free food** – not a full meal of course. Serve samples of new items that will make people want to come to your restaurant.

4. **Have prizes for the kids.**

5. **Have a magician**, local radio or TV celebrity, homecoming queen, etc.

6. **Do something involving a charity or non-profit organization** – Boy Scouts, Girl Scouts, invite the local Humane Society to bring puppies and kittens to be adopted (this will always get you publicity).

7. **Have a fire truck**, maybe give away free pictures of kids sitting in the driver's seat of the fire truck.

Use the above ideas to help you come up with a really exciting grand opening event.

#3. Finally, when you get the crowds to come, don't blow your chance to WOW them.

Be sure to amaze them, entertain them, show them a good time and convince them they will have a really **great experience** when they dine at your restaurant.

## Chapter 24

Five Quick Ways to Double Your Dessert Sales

If you're not using these five simple techniques to double your dessert sales, you're leaving a **lot** of profit on the table.

To many restaurant managers, providing desserts seems almost like providing restrooms – something they have to do. I've been to restaurants where I had to ask to see a dessert menu. Many times the servers didn't even know what kind of desserts the restaurant had.

A great dessert can make (or break) a good meal, add greatly to your guests' enjoyment – and add a lot to your bottom line profit.

Start featuring desserts and make both your guests and your accountant happy.

Below are five ways to greatly increase your dessert sales:

#1 Sell desserts *immediately* after guests are finished eating

This is the single biggest mistake restaurants make when it comes to selling desserts. They wait too long after people finish eating to offer desserts.

It's a scientifically proven fact that the stomach gets full about 20 minutes before the brain gets the message that the stomach is full. This explains why we eat too much and later can't understand why we "ate the whole thing."

Use this fact to your advantage. Immediately after people finish eating they're still hungry. Offer them dessert then and the idea is much more tempting than it will be even a few minutes later. Wait even 10 minutes after people finish eating and dessert sales will drop substantially because people will already be starting to feel full.

If there is one person in the group who is eating slowly, go ahead and offer dessert to the group even before the slow eater finishes.

To sell desserts you have to act fast!

#2 Bring your dessert selections to the table

No description of a dessert is as tempting as actually seeing the dessert. Instead of asking if anyone saved room for dessert, just bring the dessert tray around and tempt them.

Of course, don't just show the desserts. The server should describe each dessert with mouth-watering details and maybe tell the guests which one is his or her favorite, which one is very light and not filling, which one has the fewest calories, etc. Get one person to "bite" and you can probably sell everyone a dessert.

If you don't get any takers, **always** suggest sharing a dessert. Selling even one extra dessert per table will add up.

#3 Have a signature dessert

Declare one of your desserts your signature dessert. You may want to put some time and thought into this but you need to be famous for one particular dessert. Whether it's your banana pudding, key lime pie or (one of my favorites) **hot apple dumpling with homemade ice cream**, proudly feature your signature dessert.

The fact that a lot of other people like a particular dessert is a good enough reason to make most people want to try it. The fact that the restaurant is putting its name and reputation behind a particular dessert makes it even more tempting.

#4 Lock in an order for a special dessert at the same time you take the food order by offering a dessert that takes 20 minutes to prepare

When people order their meal obviously they're hungry and it's easy to make almost any dessert sound tempting, but it would be too pushy to try to get people to place an order for a dessert at the same time they order their meal. . . unless you have a **very** good "reason why."

Here's your reason why. Offer a dessert that requires about 20 minutes or so to prepare (maybe your signature dessert).

Explain that the chef prepares each of these special desserts individually and it takes about 20 minutes for the chef to do everything just right. Say to your guests, "You have to place your order now in order for the chef to have this special desert ready for you when you finish your meal." To make it even more special explain that the chef has time to prepare only a few of these each evening.

Of course, explain that it is large enough for two people if that's what it takes to sell the dessert. The special dessert can even have a slightly higher price (because it has a higher perceived value) and it becomes a very profitable item for you.

#5 Offer some unique tiny desserts

The second biggest reason people don't order desert is because most desserts are just too large, too filling and too expensive.

Solve this problem by having a selection of very small desserts for $1.95 to $2.95 each. If you can get one person to go for one of these "tiny" desserts, you will usually get everyone (or at least, several people in the group) to go for one.

I've seen this presented where the desserts are in little see-through plastic cups (to make the desserts look even more tempting).

These desserts are not expensive, not too filling and there are not even too many calories in them and they're right in front of the guests. It makes it hard to not finish the meal on a sweet note.

Some restaurants offer only the tiny desserts. Offering the tiny desserts will hurt the sale of your other desserts, so you may want to test to see whether it works better in your restaurant to offer just the tiny desserts, offer just the regular desserts or offer both tiny desserts and regular desserts.

One other option to consider is to offer the chef's special dessert that takes 20 minutes to prepare and then come back at the end of the meal with the tiny desserts to offer to people who didn't order the chef's special dessert.

Bottom line: Implement all (or at least some) of the techniques above and you can sell a lot more desserts, help your guests have a more enjoyable experience and add extra profit to your bottom line.

The tiny desserts and the chef's special dessert may take a few days to implement, but you can start using the other three techniques immediately at your next meal.

One last point to consider is that if you have people waiting for a table, you have to test to see if you would make more profit by turning tables faster or by selling more deserts.

## Chapter 25

How, When and IF You Should Move Your Successful Restaurant to a New and Larger Facility

When you're Hot you're Hot and when you're not you're not.

Don't turn your successful restaurant into a failure by making the fatal mistake many restaurants owners make when they have a great restaurant.

I'm sure you've seen it – a restaurant that is successful, has a waiting list at most meals and you can't see why.

The food is pretty good, but not the best. The building is old. The decorations and ambiance are old and outdated, but in spite of all of this the restaurant is still the "Happening Place."

Then the owner decides he needs to expand to be able to take care of more customers and be even more successful. I think sometimes the owner feels he can do no wrong. His ego is in the clouds – and maybe it should be. After all, he has been successful in building a really successful restaurant.

But what happens many times is that when he puts all of the time and money into building or buying a bigger facility, he ends up not getting the extra business he expected. In fact, in many cases he loses a lot of his regular customers.

The new place is just not the same

Maybe it's not as convenient (especially if it moved even as much as a mile away from the original location). Maybe a lot of the original staff are no longer there.

Many times your existing customers can't even tell you why they come there so often. Maybe it's just habit. But. . .

When you have the right mix and everything is working almost like magic, be very, very careful about trying to improve things.

There could be a ton of reasons, but it's just not the same place the original customers loved. Don't let this happen to you.

Consider these alternatives

Consider adding an outside seating area or adding on another dining area inside. Maybe make the kitchen larger if that would help you serve people faster. Maybe add a take-out window and promote it to help take some of the load off the dining area.

Bottom line concerning moving your restaurant: Look at a LOT of options before you decide to move your successful restaurant into a new or larger place. It could be a disaster. I've seen it happen many times.

## Chapter 26

Some Final Thoughts on Marketing Your Restaurant

Now you're armed with more than enough restaurant marketing information and low-cost marketing techniques to **turn your restaurant into a cash-generating-machine.**

All you have to do is go apply these techniques. And the best part is that you don't have to do everything at once.

Do a little bit each day and the profits will start rolling in. Most restaurant owners and managers don't spend even a few minutes a month on their marketing and when they do, it's usually spent listening to some smooth-talking ad sales person who is promising them the moon.

Follow the techniques I've outlined and soon you can be enjoying life with your super-successful restaurant and be working only four hours a day. Who knows, maybe you can reach the plateau described in the book we talked about in the Introduction, *The 4-Hour Workweek.*

Just remember to work "<u>on</u> your restaurant" and NOT "<u>in</u> your restaurant" and also keep the point in mind that you can't make $100,000 a year doing $10 an hour work.

Your primary job is to market your restaurant.

A successful restaurant owner told me recently, "My success and profits are directly related to my knowledge of marketing. The more I learn about marketing, the more my profits go up each year."

Rather than giving you a long essay on why information and knowledge are important to the success of your restaurant, I want to give you some one-line comments from several (rich and successful) people to stimulate your thinking.

I will throw in a few of my own comments and observations along the way.

I'm telling you this to motivate you and to convince you to spend more time reading, studying and most important, implementing what you have learned from this site.

Here are the powerful statements I want you to consider:

"Knowledge may be expensive, but ignorance is even more expensive."

In business knowledge is directly related to wealth. Maybe that's why. . .

Here is one of my favorite sayings that I keep above my desk.

"I can't know everything, but I can learn anything."

You can't just copy what the big chain restaurants are doing or what your competitors are doing – because. . .

"Conventional wisdom is usually wrong."

Most big profits are made when someone does something unconventional.

"Think outside the box"

This phrase has been so over-used, I hated to use it, but it's an important concept to learn. I very seldom get a good idea sitting behind my desk. I get my great ideas when I'm out experiencing things – seeing problems, solutions, people's frustrations, innovations, etc.

You not only have to **think** outside the box, you have to **be** outside the **box** or in other words, outside of your restaurant to get fresh ideas.

The richest and smartest people in the restaurant business don't always have the best answers, but they do always ask the right questions.

How much time are you spending asking the right questions about your restaurant?

For any problem there is always at least one simple and obvious solution. . . that doesn't work.

Ray Kroc (the founder of McDonald's) was obviously in a very competitive business. How did he manage to be so successful? Ray Kroc said,

"We invent faster than they can copy."

Your marketing knowledge (and the implementation of this knowledge) is your **only** competitive advantage. This book gives you the **"knowledge."**

Now it's your job to use this knowledge to drive a starving crowd to your restaurant.

You can accomplish everything described in this book **working only 4-hours a day** – that is IF you quit doing all of the $10 an hour work you have been doing and devote most of your time to marketing your restaurant. Someone else can do almost everything else you have been doing, but only **you** can successfully market your restaurant.

My closing advice:

Of all the ideas and techniques you have learned in this book, don't forget the most important one of all concerning your advertising and marketing endeavors. . .

Track it or Trash it

Contact Jerry Minchey

Jerry's weekly restaurant marketing articles and a free restaurant marketing *Tip of the Week* can be obtained from Jerry's restaurant marketing website at:

www.MarketingYourRestaurant.com

If you want more detailed information about how to market your business on the Internet using Google and the other search engines, go to Jerry's **Search Engine University** website at:

www.SearchEngineU.com

For information on upcoming seminars or to book Jerry Minchey for private coaching or speaking engagements...

Email Jerry at JMinchey@Gmail.com

Made in the USA
Lexington, KY
17 May 2015